VERSEFORM

VERSEFORM

A COMPARATIVE
BIBLIOGRAPHY

T. V. F. Brogan

THE JOHNS HOPKINS UNIVERSITY PRESS
Baltimore and London

The Johns Hopkins University Press
701 West 40th Street
Baltimore, Maryland 21211
The Johns Hopkins Press Ltd., London

The paper used in this publication meets the minimum requirements of American National
Standard for Information Sciences—Permanence of Paper for Printed Library Materials,
ANSI Z39.48–1984.

LIBRARY OF CONGRESS CATALOGING-IN-PUBLICATION DATA

Brogan, T. V. F. (Terry V. F.)
Verseform : a comparative bibliography.

Includes index.
1. Versification—Bibliography.   I. Title.
Z7156.V6B76   1988   016.8081   88-45406
[PN1031]
ISBN 0-8018-3362-0 (alk. paper)

Of versifying there are two sorts, the one ancient, the other modern.

— S I D N E Y

CONTENTS

PREFACE

For twenty years now there has been unprecedented interest in the United States in the form and forms of poetry. After a century of experimentation with free verse—which, as W. H. Auden remarked, is far harder to write, at its best, than the metrical verse that preceded it—poets have taken renewed interest in more traditional forms. This is not hard to understand: the free-verse movement itself was not, in retrospect, so much a reaction to a set of forms as a reaction to the social conventions and attitudes that legitimized them and held them in place. But those attitudes have manifestly gone, gone altogether. Therefore poets, who are now as much as in Homer's day, or ever, on the lookout for new devices, new verbal modes, may turn to look at traditional forms as if new—for they are new, in a very real sense. Stripped by time of much of their associative baggage, these old-new forms become simply possibilities, opportunities, strategies—ways of proceeding.

Critical interest in poetic form has also been renewed and intensified over the past twenty years. By the mid-sixties, the influence of the maturing science of linguistics had made itself felt in poetics as some of the most experienced linguists in the world—one thinks of Roman Jakobson first, but there were many—turned their attention to verse, the oldest and most prestigious form of composition known to humanity.

In 1981 I tried to collect, in one place, some of the voluminous work on verseform, so that someone coming to the field for the first time could get a coherent sense of the field as a whole, could see how it was laid out, or organized, could see how much work had been done on each subject or area, and could gauge how good that work was. A reader would then have a sense of context, when reading a book or article on a specialized topic, and would have, perhaps even more importantly, a sense of the basic structure of the theory, the basic concepts and terms that have been developed for talking about verse and its structure. Someone not coming to the field for the first time would still find the book useful for supplying references not previously known or for making cross-references hitherto unseen. That book was entitled, a little awkwardly, *English Versification, 1570–1980: A Reference Guide,* also published by Johns Hopkins. It was intended to be comprehensive for English—I cited and discussed every study known to have been published between 1570 and 1980 on English poetry from *Beowulf* up to the present— and selective for all the other major poetries of the world (about thirty)—these studies being listed in an appendix amounting to almost a third of the book.

The book was noticed and, I would like to think, valued; even more important, I hope, it was used. It brought a great deal of material into one locus and gave it shape. Still, inevitably it turned out to be a very large book, too expensive for the average reader or student to buy, and thus fated by its nature to inhabit the reference rooms of libraries. Too, *English Versification* listed, at least for English, every study known, the good with the bad, the broad with the narrow, the great with the small. There was much wheat but also much chaff. I wanted some means of sifting out the less consequential, dated, and minor work, some means of highlighting the more important work, within smaller compass, in a more convenient and attractive format, and at a more reasonable price. That is the rationale for the present work.

In this book I collect what I see as the basic and most important work for the study of verseform. Not necessarily the most conspicuous work, mind you, for in some cases the biggest and oldest studies are also the least reliable. There are points in the field where more is conveyed of importance in a ten-page article than in a three-hundred-page book. Consequently, my regard has been simply to list the standard reference works and the best critical works for every major verse tradition in the world. I do not give extensive or evaluative commentary; that is precluded by the principle of selectivity which is the rationale for the book. I do give factual information of a bibliographic nature—how many essays are in an anthology, for example, or the nature and scope of other bibliographies besides mine.

When I conceived this book—that is, its readers and the uses it would be put to, hence the needs it would have to fill—I imagined that most readers would come to it wanting information on a particular topic (such as rhythm or onomatopoeia) or on one particular national poetry (such as French). These ends are mutually contradictory, at least insofar as making reference books is concerned; but as far as using reference books is concerned, they are simply facts of life. So I designed the book to have a double format in order to try to satisfy both. For example, in the chapter on "Rhythm" in part 1, the reader will find listed the most important studies of poetic rhythm, regardless of language. Every reader will ignore one or another of these, but some others will be immediately interesting and, if pursued, will lead to a much wider conception of the topic than if one had merely read studies of rhythm in one language only. Hence the chapters in part 1 are entirely comparative in scope. In this, this little book is rather audacious, despite appearances; I mean to encourage, by the very design of the book, a comparative approach to the study of poetry.

In part 2, works are organized by language. Here I set forth the standard references for each verse tradition: bibliographies specific to each poetry, encyclopedias and dictionaries of poetry or prosody, histories of the verse, stanza indexes, and specialized studies. There are no redundancies between part 1 and part 2—a given work appears once in the entire book—so cross-references between the parts are frequent, and they are given in an improved format over the one I used in *English Versification*. A reader who wants to know about the rhythm of French poetry, for example, can look into the chapter on "French," where the more general studies of French verse are cited and where studies of rhythm are cross-referenced to the chapter on "Rhythm"; or she can look into the latter chapter, where all the major studies of poetic rhythm are cited, some of which treat French specifically, with cross-references to more generalized studies of French prosody in the chapter on French which include discussion of rhythm. Either direction will work.

Using the cross-references will be valuable, then, but browsing more widely will be equally of value if not more so. This is a relatively short book, so the reader who is willing to scan several chapters beyond the one of immediate interest is sure to find other valuable items that even the most sophisticated cross-referencing could never entirely capture.

Finally, I have brought the book entirely up to date. The lists in *English Versification* stopped at 1980, but I have broadened my researches since that time, all of which work has been brought to bear on the present book. Indeed, several excellent studies have appeared within the past year; these are dutifully noted herein.

In short, this book is a list of the standard and best studies of poetic form in all the major languages of the world, brought completely up to date and organized in a way that I hope will be useful for finding good work on any topic or national poetry quickly and conveniently. For more extensive references, one can then go to *English Versification* or to the several other specialized bibliographies listed in part 2 of this work.

I owe thanks to my very able assistants, especially Rose Gallagher, who helped with the proofs.

ONE

STRUCTURES, DEVICES, FORMS

GENERAL REFERENCES

BIBLIOGRAPHIES

Seven sources whose references to works on prosody are general or comparative in scope are listed below with comment. More specialized bibliographies of the prosodies of particular languages (e.g., English, French) are listed in the various chapters of part 2.

1 *Arts & Humanities Citation Index*. 1976– (quarterly).

Search for prosodic key words (i.e., the names of meters or stanza forms) in the *Permuterm Index;* authors' names listed under each term there refer to entries in the *Citation Index*. Because it appears quarterly, *AHCI* is much more current than the *MLA International Bibliography* [6], though neither is particularly easy to use.

2 Brogan, T. V. F. *English Versification, 1570–1980: A Reference Guide with a Global Appendix*. Baltimore: Johns Hopkins University Press, 1981. 794 pp.

Not aptly titled; the book provides references to about 4,000 studies of English prosody published after 1570, though the studies cover Old and Middle English poetry as well as Modern. In other words, the dates in the title refer to the publication dates of critical works, not to the dates of the poems themselves. The appendix cites about 2,000 more studies of all other major languages in the world. Annotations, sometimes lengthy.

3 *Eidos: The International Prosody Bulletin*. 1984– (quarterly).

The annual bibliography of "Studies of Verseform," which first appeared in 1984, is retroactive to 1979 so as to extend the coverage in Brogan [2].

4 Gayley, C. M., and F. N. Scott. *An Introduction to the Methods and Materials of Literary Criticism*. Boston: Ginn, 1901.

Now nearly forgotten but unjustly so: a sixty-page "General Note" at the end cites nearly 1,000 sources in seventeen languages.

5 *Linguistic Bibliography/Bibliographie linguistique*. Utrecht, 1937– (annual).

S.v. "Prosodie, Métrique, Versification."

6 *MLA International Bibliography of Books and Articles on the Modern Languages and Literatures*. 1920– (annual; now 5 vols.).

Enormous in size and slow to appear, the *MLA*'s hyperspecific subject headings make it unreasonably difficult for average users to learn to use. The subject index appearing after 1980 is very useful though heavily redundant. Use [1] when possible.

7 *Style*. 1967– (quarterly).

The annual bibliography of works on style and stylistics includes works on prosody; it is best read in its entirety.

GENERAL STUDIES, ANTHOLOGIES

8 Beare, William. *Latin Verse and European Song: A Study in Accent and Rhythm*. London: Methuen, 1957; rpt. New York: Humanities, 1979. 296 pp.

9 Chatman, Seymour, and Samuel R. Levin, eds. *Essays on the Language of Literature*. Boston: Houghton Mifflin, 1967. 450 pp.

Contains thirty-one papers on sound, metrics, grammar, form, and style.

10 Conway, Gilbert. *A Treatise on Versification*. London: Longmans, 1878. 113 pp.

11 Cremante, Renzo, and Mario Pazzaglia, eds. *La Metrica*. 2nd ed. Bologna: Il Mulino, 1976.

A large collection of general essays on verse theory (a number are translations of previous publications) and on Italian metrics; bibliography.

12 Du Meril, Edelestand. *Essai philosophique sur le principe et les formes de la versification*. Paris, 1841. 230 pp.

❖ Ernst, Ulrich, and Peter-Erich Neuser, eds. [112].

13 Evans, R. W. *A Treatise on Versification*. London, 1852. 169 pp.

14 Fónagy, Ivan. "Communication in Poetry." *Word* 17 (1961): 194–218.

15 ———. "Form and Function of Poetic Language." *Diogenes* 51 (1965): 72–110.

16 Fowler, Roger, ed. *Essays on Style and Language: Linguistic and Critical Approaches to Literary Style*. London: Routledge & Kegan Paul, 1966. 188 pp.

Ten essays.

17 Freeman, Donald C., ed. *Essays in Modern Stylistics*. London: Methuen, 1981. 416 pp.

Sixteen essays, some prosodic.

18 Frye, Northrop, ed. *Sound and Poetry: English Institute Essays, 1956*. New York: Columbia University Press, 1957.

Introduction and six papers on music and poetry and on sound and meaning in poetry.

19 Groot, A. Willem de. *Allgemene Versleer* [General Prosody]. The Hague: Servire, 1946. 157 pp.

20 Gross, Harvey, ed. *The Structure of Verse: Modern Essays on Prosody*. 2nd ed. New York: Ecco, 1979. 293 pp.

Introduction, fifteen essays, glossary, and bibliography.

21 Habermann, Paul, and Klaus Kanzog. "Vers, Verslehre, Vers und Prosa." In *Reallexikon* [1182], 2nd ed., vol. 4, pp. 677–98.

22 Hollander, John. *Vision and Resonance: Two Senses of Poetic Form*. 2nd ed. New Haven: Yale University Press, 1985. 322 pp.

Twelve essays, appendix, and afterword.

23 Jakobson, Roman. "Concluding Statement: Linguistics and Poetics." In Sebeok, ed. [57], pp. 350–77; rpt. in Chatman and Levin, eds. [9], pp. 296–322; rpt. in *Poetry of Grammar and Grammar of Poetry* [269], pp. 18–51.

❖ ———. *Early Slavic Paths and Crossroads* [1374].

24 ———. "My Metrical Sketches: A Retrospect." *Linguistics* 17, nos. 3–4 (1979): 267–99; rpt. in *On Verse* [25], pp. 569–601.

25 ———. *On Verse: Its Masters and Explorers*. Vol. 5 of Jakobson's *Selected Writings*. The Hague: Mouton, 1979. 623 pp.

❖ ———. *Poetry of Grammar and Grammar of Poetry* [269].

❖ ———. *Slavic Epic Studies* [1376].

26 Jakobson, Roman, and Krystyna Pomorska. *Dialogues*. Paris: Flammarion, 1980; English trans. Christian Hubert. Cambridge, Mass.: MIT Press, 1983.

27 Jakobson, Roman, and Linda Waugh. "The Spell of Speech Sounds." *The Sound Shape of Language*. Bloomington: Indiana University Press, 1979. Pp. 177–231.

28 Johnson, Wendell Stacy. "Some Functions of Poetic Form." *JAAC* 13 (1955): 496–506.

29 Ker, W. P. *Form and Style in Poetry*. Ed. R. W. Chapman. London: Macmillan, 1928; rpt. New York: Russell & Russell, 1966.

30 Kiparsky, Paul. "The Role of Linguistics in a Theory of Poetry." *Daedalus* 102 (1973): 231–44.

31 Koch, Walter A. *Recurrence and a Three-Modal Approach to Poetry*. The Hague: Mouton, 1966. 55 pp.

32 Kreuzer, Helmut, and Rul Gunzenhäuser, eds. *Mathematik und Dichtung: Versuche zur Frage einer exakten Literaturwissenschaft*. 4th ed. Munich: Nymphenburg, 1971. 363 pp.

Introduction, twenty-one papers, and bibliography.

33 Kurylowicz, Jerzy. "The Linguistic Foundations of Metre." *Biuletin Polskiego Towarzystwa Jazykoznawczego* 34 (1976): 63–72.

34 ———. *Metrik und Sprachgeschichte*. Wroclaw: Wydaw. polskiej akad. nauk., 1975. 254 pp.

Collects thirteen of his essays on comparative metrics.

35 La Drière, J. Craig. "The Comparative Method in the Study of Prosody." *Comparative Literature: Proceedings of the Second Congress of the International Comparative Literature Association*. Ed. W. P. Friedrich. Chapel Hill: University of North Carolina Press, 1959. Vol. 1, pp. 160–75.

36 La Drière, J. Craig, and T. V. F. Brogan. "Prosody." *Princeton Handbook* [56], pp. 218–23.

37 Levin, Samuel R. "The Conventions of Poetry." *Literary Style; A Symposium*. Ed. Seymour Chatman. London: Oxford University Press, 1971. Pp. 171–93.

38 ———. *Linguistic Structures in Poetry*. The Hague: Mouton, 1962. 64 pp.

39 Levý, Jiří. "The Meanings of Form and the Forms of Meaning." In *Poetics II* [53], pp. 45–60; rpt. in Levý [1382], pp. 97–109.

40 ———, ed. *Teorie Verše I/Theory of Verse I/Teorija stixa I. Proceedings of the First Versological Conference, 13–16 May 1964*. Brno: Universita J. E. Purkyně, 1966. 269 pp.

Twenty-eight papers.

41 Levý, Jiří, and Karel Palas, eds. *Teorie Verše II/Theory of Verse II/Teorija stixa II. Proceedings of the Second Versological Conference, 18–20 October 1966*. Brno: Universita J. E. Purkyně, 1968. 95 pp.

Twenty-one papers.

42 Lotman, Jurij M. "Elements and Levels of the Paradigmatics of the Artistic Text." *The Structure of the Artistic Text*. Ann Arbor: University of Michigan Press, 1977. Pp. 94–197.

43 Lotz, John. "Elements of Versification." In Wimsatt, ed. [60], pp. 1–21.

44 Marcus, Solomon. "On Types of Meters of a Poem and Their Informational Energy." *Semiotica* 4 (1971): 31–36.

45 "Metrica." *Enciclopedia italiana*. Rome: Istituto della Enciclopedia italiana, 1929–39. Vol. 23 (1934), pp. 102–13.

Seven verse-traditions are surveyed: Oriental, Classical, Medieval, French, Italian, German, and Slavic.

46 Meyer, Herman. "On the Spirit of Verse." *The Disciplines of Criticism*. Ed. Peter Demetz et al. New Haven: Yale University Press, 1968. Pp. 331–47.

47 Mitford, William. *An Inquiry into the Principles of Harmony in Language and the Mechanism of Verse, Ancient and Modern*. 2nd ed. London, 1804.

48 Murray, Gilbert. "Metre." *The Classical Tradition in Poetry*. Cambridge, Mass.: Harvard University Press, 1927. Pp. 80–121.

49 Nowottny, Winifred. *The Language Poets Use*. 2nd ed. London: Athlone, 1965. 225 pp.

50 Olson, Elder. "General Prosody: Rhythmik, Metrik, Harmonics." Ph.D. diss., University of Chicago, 1938.

51 Pighi, G. B. *Studi di ritmica e metrica*. Turin: Bottega d'Erasmo, 1970. 633 pp.

52 *Poetics, Poetyka, Poetika: First International Conference on Work-in-Progress Devoted to Problems of Poetics, Warsaw 1960*. Ed. Donald Davie et al. Warsaw: Polish Scientific Publishers, 1961.

Sixty-two papers and abstracts in several languages; bibliography.

53 *Poetics, Poetyka, Poetika: Third International Conference on Work-in-Progress Devoted to Problems of Poetics, Warsaw 1964*. Ed. Roman Jakobson et al. The Hague: Mouton, 1966.

Eighteen papers on Slavic and comparative metrics; bibliography.

54 Polivanov, E. D. "The General Phonetic Principle of Any Poetic Technique." *Selected Works*. Ed. A. A. Leontev. The Hague: Mouton, 1974. Pp. 350–68.

55 Preminger, Alex, Frank J. Warnke, and O. B. Hardison, Jr., eds. *Princeton Encyclopedia of Poetry and Poetics*. Enl. ed. Princeton: Princeton University Press, 1974. 992 pp.

56 ———. *The Princeton Handbook of Poetic Terms*. Princeton: Princeton University Press, 1986. 309 pp.

Ten new entries and a new "Select Reading List" covering genres, meters, and forms.

57 Sebeok, Thomas A., ed. *Style in Language*. Cambridge, Mass.: MIT Press, 1960. 470 pp.

Includes twenty-two papers or abstracts, discussion, and six summary opening and closing statements from the perspectives of linguistics, psychology, and literary criticism, all presented at the 1958 Conference on Style held at Indiana University.

❖ Smith, G. S., ed. *Metre, Rhythm, Stanza, Rhyme* [1395].

58 Stevens, John. *Words and Music in the Middle Ages: Song, Narrative, Dance and Drama, 1050–1350*. Cambridge: Cambridge University Press, 1986. 554 pp.

❖ Valéry, Paul. *The Art of Poetry* [1171].

59 Wellek, René, and Austin Warren. "Euphony, Rhythm, and Metre." *Theory of Literature*. 3rd ed., rev. New York: Harcourt, Brace & World, 1963. Pp. 158–73.

60 Wimsatt, W. K., Jr., ed. *Versification: Major Language Types: Sixteen Essays.* New York: New York University Press, 1972. 252 pp.

Fifteen essays survey all the major national poetries; editor's introduction.

61 Winn, James A. *Unsuspected Eloquence: A History of the Relations between Poetry and Music.* New Haven: Yale University Press, 1981. 381 pp.

SOUND PATTERNING

GENERAL STUDIES

62 Ahl, Frederick. *Metaformations: Soundplay and Wordplay in Ovid and Other Classical Poets.* Ithaca: Cornell University Press, 1984.

63 Bishop, Lloyd O. "Euphony: A New Method of Analysis." *Language and Style* 18 (1985): 342–62.

64 ———. *In Search of Style: Essays in French Literary Stylistics.* Charlottesville: University Press of Virginia, 1982. Chap. 4.

65 Burke, Kenneth. "On Musicality in Verse, as Illustrated by Some Lines of Coleridge." *Poetry* 57 (1940): 31–40; rpt. in his *The Philosophy of Literary Form.* Rev. ed. New York: Vintage, 1957, 1967. Pp. 296–304.

66 Chapman, Raymond. *The Treatment of Sounds in Language and Literature.* Oxford: Basil Blackwell, 1984. 262 pp.

❖ Chatman and Levin, eds. [9], part 1.

67 Chesters, Graham. *Some Functions of Sound Repetition in "Les Fleurs du Mal."* Hull: University of Hull Press, 1975.

68 Ehrstine, John W. "Patterns of Sound in Anglo-Saxon Poetry." *Research Studies of the State College of Washington* 33 (1965): 151–62.

69 Hymes, Dell. "Phonological Aspects of Style: Some English Sonnets." In Sebeok, ed. [57], pp. 109–31 (cf. 412–13); rpt. in Chatman and Levin, eds. [9], pp. 33–53.

70 Kintgen, Eugene R., Jr. "Echoic Repetition in Old English Poetry." *Neuphilologische Mitteilungen* 75 (1974): 202–23.

71 ———. " 'Lif,' 'Lof,' 'Leof,' 'Lufu,' and 'Geleafa' in Old English Poetry." *Neuphilologische Mitteilungen* 78 (1977): 309–16.

72 La Drière, J. Craig. "Structure, Sound, and Meaning." In Frye, ed. [18], pp. 85–108.

73 Lynch, James J. "The Tonality of Lyric Poetry: An Experiment in Method." *Word* 9 (1953): 211–24.

74 McCreesh, Thomas P. "Poetic Sound Patterns in Proverbs 10–29." *DAI* 43, 1A (1982): 155 (Catholic University of America). 235 pp.

75 Masson, David I. "Poetic Sound-Patterning Reconsidered." *Proceedings of the Leeds Philological and Literary Society, Literary and Historical Section* 16 (1976): 61–124.

76 ———. "Sound in Poetry." *Princeton Encyclopedia* [55], pp. 784–90.

77 ———. "Thematic Analysis of Sounds in Poetry." *Proceedings of the Leeds Philological and Literary Society, Literary and Historical Section* 9 (1960): 133–47; rpt. in Chatman and Levin, eds. [10], pp. 54–68.

78 ———. "Word and Sound in Yeats's 'Byzantium.' " *ELH* 20 (1953): 136–60.

79 Newton, Robert P. *Vowel Undersong: Studies of Vocalic Timbre and Chroneme Patterning in German Lyric Poetry*. The Hague: Mouton, 1981. 456 pp.

80 Oras, Ants. "Spenser and Milton: Some Parallels and Contrasts in the Handling of Sound." In Frye, ed. [18], pp. 109–33; rpt. in Chatman and Levin, eds. [9], pp. 19–32.

81 Smith, Chard Powers. *Pattern and Variation in Poetry*. New York: Scribner's, 1932.

82 Stanford, W. B. *The Sound of Greek: Studies in the Greek Theory and Practice of Euphony*. Berkeley and Los Angeles: University of California Press, 1967. 177 pp.

83 Thompson, Ewa M. "Sound Correlations in Verse." *Language Quarterly* 8 (1969): 39–42.

❖ Wilkinson, L. P. [691], part 1.

ALLITERATION, ASSONANCE, CONSONANCE

84 Adams, Percy G. *Graces of Harmony: Alliteration, Assonance, and Consonance in Eighteenth-Century British Poetry*. Athens: University of Georgia Press, 1967. 253 pp.

85 Allen, John D. *Quantitative Studies in Prosody*. Johnson City: East Tennessee State University Press, 1968. Part 1.

86 Diamond, Celia B. "Alliterative Figurations, Syntax, and Meaning in Old English Poetry." *DAI* 31, 10A (1971): 5395 (Pennsylvania).

87 Douglas-Lithgow, R. A. "Anglo-Saxon Alliterative Poetry (A.D. 449 to A.D. 1150)"; "Early-English Alliterative Poetry (A.D. 1150 to A.D. 1550)"; "English Alliteration from Chaucer to Milton." *Transactions of the Royal Society of Literature*, ser. 2, 15 (1893): 178–220; 16 (1894): 99–134; 18 (1897): 115–50.

88 Goldsmith, Ulrich K. "Words out of a Hat? Alliteration and Assonance in Shakespeare's Sonnets." *JEGP* 49 (1950): 33–48.

89 Kim, James. "A Study of Some Alliterative and Assonantal Features of the Language of [Hebrew] Proverbs." *DAI* 36, 5A (1975): 2790 (Brandeis).

90 Leavitt, Jay A. "On the Measurement of Alliteration in Poetry." *Computers and the Humanities* 10 (1976): 333–42.

91 Lewis, Richard A. "Alliteration and Old English Metre." *Medium Ævum* 41 (1973): 119–30.

92 ———. "Plurilinear Alliteration in Old English Poetry." *Texas Studies in Literature and Language* 16 (1975): 589–602.

93 McClumpha, Charles F. *The Alliteration of Chaucer.* Leipzig, 1888. 56 pp.

94 Oras, Ants. "Surrey's Technique of Phonetic Echoes: A Method and Its Background." *JEGP* 50 (1951): 289–308.

95 Pirkhofer, Anton M. " 'A Pretty Pleasing Pricket': On the Use of Alliteration in Shakespeare's Sonnets." *Shakespeare Quarterly* 14 (1963): 3–14.

96 Scholz, Martin. "Die Alliteration in der altprovenzalischen Lyrik." *Zeitschrift für Romanische Philologie* 37 (1913): 385–426.

97 Spencer, Virginia E. *Alliteration in Spenser's Poetry Discussed and Compared with the Alliteration as Employed by Drayton and Daniel.* Zurich, 1898. 144 pp.

98 Wheelock, James T. S. "Alliterative Functions in the *Divina Commedia*." *Lingua e Stile* 13 (1978): 373–404.

RHYME

99 Abernathy, Robert. "Rhymes, Non-Rhymes, and Antirhymes." *To Honor Roman Jakobson: Essays on the Occasion of His Seventieth Birthday.* 3 vols. The Hague: Mouton, 1967. Vol. 1, pp. 1–14.

100 Beum, Robert. "The Rhyme in *Samson Agonistes*." *Texas Studies in Literature and Language* 4 (1962): 177–82.

101 ———. "Yeats the Rhymer." In Beum [784], pp. 86–105.

102 Billy, Dominique. "La Nomenclature des rimes." *Poétique,* no. 57 (1984): 64–75.

103 Birkenhauer, Renate. *Reimpoetik—am Beispiel Stefan Georges.* Halle: Max Niemeyer, 1983. 316 pp.

104 Bolinger, Dwight L. "Rime, Assonance, and Morpheme Analysis." *Word* 6 (1950): 117–36.

❖ Brogan, T. V. F. [2], pp. 77–97.

105 Clark, Arthur Melville. "The Rhyming Ancients"; "The Difficulty of Rhyming"; "Rhyme and No Rhyme." *Studies in Literary Modes*. Edinburgh: Oliver & Boyd, 1945. Pp. 149–65, 166–77, 178–210.

106 Combs, Bruce E. "A Linguistic Analysis of Rime." *DAI* 30, 11A (1970): 4963 (Oregon).

107 Cornulier, Benoît de. "La Rime n'est pas une marqué du fin de vers." *Poétique*, no. 46 (1981): 247–56.

108 De Selincourt, B. "Rhyme in English Poetry." *Essays and Studies* 7 (1921): 7–29.

109 Diekhoff, John S. "Rhyme in *Paradise Lost*." *PMLA* 49 (1934): 539–43.

110 Draper, John W. *Rhyme in the Pacific*. Morgantown: West Virginia University, 1959. 29 pp.

111 Eekman, Thomas. *The Realm of Rime: A Study of Rime in the Poetry of the Slavs*. Amsterdam: Hakkert, 1974. 364 pp.

❖ Elwell-Sutton, L. P. [1460]. "Rhyme," pp. 223–42.

112 Ernst, Ulrich, and Peter-Erich Neuser, eds. *Die Genese der europäischen Endreimdichtung*. Darmstadt: Wissenschaftliche Buchgesellschaft, 1977. 524 pp.

Includes twenty-two papers, a long synoptic introduction ("Bausteine zu einer Geschichte der Reimtheorie: Dokumentation und Analyse"), and a bibliography on the importation and diffusion of rhyme in the European poetries.

113 Freymond, E. "Über den reichen Reim bei altfranzösischen Dichtern bis zum Anfang des XIV Jahrhundert." *Zeitschrift für Romanische Philologie* 6 (1882): 1–36, 177–215.

114 Guggenheimer, Eva H. *Rhyme Effects and Rhyming Figures: A Comparative Study of Sound Repetitions in the Classics, with Emphasis on Latin Poetry*. The Hague: Mouton, 1972. 236 pp.

115 Habermann, Paul. "Reim." *Reallexikon*, 1st ed. [1181], vol. 3, pp. 25–44.

116 Herbert, T. Walter. "The Grammar of Rimes." *Sewanee Review* 48 (1940): 362–77.

117 ———. "Near-Rimes and Paraphones." *Sewanee Review* 45 (1937): 433–52.

❖ Heusler, Andreas [1185], parts 3, 5.

118 Hill, Archibald A. "A Phonological Description of Poetic Ornaments." *Language and Style* 2 (1969): 99–123.

119 Hollander, John. "Rhyme and the True Calling of Words." In Hollander [22], pp. 117–34.

❖ Kastner, L. E. [1106], chap. 3.

120 Lanz, Henry. *The Physical Basis of Rhyme: An Essay on the Aesthetics of Sound.* Stanford: Stanford University Press, 1931. 365 pp.

121 Masui, Michio. *The Structure of Chaucer's Rime Words.* Tokyo: Kenkyusha, 1964. 371 pp.

❖ Meyer, Wilhelm [709], vol. 1, chap. 2.

122 Molino, Jean, and Joëlle Tamine. "Des Rimes, et quelques raisons." *Poétique,* no. 52 (1982): 487–98; reply: 499–508.

❖ Morier, Henri [1104].

123 Nagel, Bert. *Das Reimproblem in der deutschen Dichtung vom Otfridvers zum freien Vers.* Berlin: Schmitt, 1985. 177 pp.

124 Nemoianu, Virgil. "Levels of Study in the Semantics of Rhyme." *Style* 5 (1971): 246–64.

125 Ness, Frederic W. *The Use of Rhyme in Shakespeare's Plays.* New Haven: Yale University Press, 1941. 168 pp.

126 Norden, Eduard. *Die Antike Kunstprosa.* 5th ed. 2 vols. Leipzig and Darmstadt: Wissenschaftliche Buchgesellschaft, 1958.

127 Oras, Ants. "Echoing Verse Endings in *Paradise Lost.*" *South Atlantic Studies for S. E. Leavitt.* Ed. Thomas B. Stroup and S. A. Stoudemire. Washington, D.C.: Scarecrow, 1953. Pp. 175–90.

128 Owen, Charles A., Jr. " 'Thy Drasty Ryming.' " *Studies in Philology* 63 (1966): 533–64.

❖ Patterson, Warner Forrest [1107].

129 Perloff, Marjorie. *Rhyme and Meaning in the Poetry of Yeats.* The Hague: Mouton, 1970. 249 pp.

130 Pretzel, Ulrich. *Frühgeschichte des deutschen Reims.* Palaestra, vol. 220. Leipzig: Becker and Erler, 1941. 272 pp,

131 Pszczolowska, Lucylla. *Rym.* Wroclaw: Ossolineum, 1970.

132 Rankin, J. W. "Rhythm and Rime before the Norman Conquest." *PMLA* 36 (1921): 401–28.

133 ———. "Rime and Reason." *PMLA* 44 (1929): 997–1004.

134 Rickert, William E. "Rhyme Terms." *Style* 12 (1978): 35–46.

135 Ryder, Frank G. "How Rhymed Is a Poem?" *Word* 19 (1963): 310–21.

❖ Saintsbury, George [767], vol. 1, app. B; vol. 3, app. 4.

❖ Schipper, Jakob [768].

136 Schweikle, Günther. "Reim." *Reallexikon,* 2nd ed. [1182], vol. 3, pp. 403–31.

❖ Scott, Clive [1162], chap. 4.

137 Shapiro, Michael. "Rhyme." *Asymmetry: An Inquiry into the Linguistic Structure of Poetry*. Amsterdam: North Holland, 1976. Pp. 135–203.

❖ Thieme, Hugo P. [1101], chap. 8 and subject index, pp. 376–80.

Full survey of French works to 1914.

138 Törnqvist, Nils. "Zur Geschichte des Wortes Reim" [in Celtic, Germanic, and Romance]. *Humanistika Vetenskapssamfundet i Lund, Årsberättelse* 3 (1934–35): 67–131.

139 Wesle, Karl. *Frühmittelhochdeutsche Reimstudien*. Jena: Frommann, 1925.

140 Wesling, Donald. *The Chances of Rhyme: Device and Modernity*. Berkeley and Los Angeles: University of California Press, 1980. 170 pp.

141 Wimsatt, W. K., Jr. "One Relation of Rhyme to Reason: Alexander Pope." *MLQ* 5 (1944): 323–38; rpt. in *The Verbal Icon*. Lexington: University of Kentucky Press, 1954. Pp. 153–68.

142 Worth, Dean S. "Roman Jakobson and the Study of Rhyme." *Roman Jakobson: Echoes of His Scholarship*. Ed. Daniel Armstrong and C. H. Van Schooneveld. Lisse: Peter de Ridder, 1977. Pp. 515–33.

143 Wyld, Henry C. *Studies in English Rhymes from Surrey to Pope*. London: John Murray, 1923.

144 Zhirmunskij, Viktor M. *Rifma, ee istoriia i teoriia*. Petrograd, 1923.

ORIGIN OF RHYME

145 Croke, Alexander. *An Essay on the origin, progress, and decline of rhyming latin verse; with many specimens*. Oxford: D. A. Talboys, 1828. 142 pp.

146 Draper, John W. "The Origin of Rhyme." *Revue de Littérature Comparée* 31 (1957): 74–85; 39 (1965): 452–53.

147 Gray, Thomas. "Observations on the Pseudo-Rhythmus." Sect. 3 of "Metrum" in *Works*. Ed. Edmund Gosse. 4 vols. New York, 1885. Vol 1, pp. 323–409.

148 Grimm, Wilhelm Karl. "Zur Geschichte des Reims" [1852]. *Kleinere Schriften*. Gütersloh, 1887. Vol. 4, pp. 125–341.

149 Sedgwick, W. B. "The Origin of Rhyme." *Revue Bénédictine* 36 (1924): 330–46.

150 Swift, Theophilus. "Essay on the Rise and Progress of Rhime." *Transactions of the Royal Irish Academy* 9 (1803): 3–79.

151 Turner, Sharon. "An Inquiry Respecting the Early Use of Rhyme." *Archaeologia* 14 (1808): 168–204.

152 Whitehall, Harold. "Rhyme: Sources and Diffusion." *Ibadan* 25 (1968): 21–26.

ONOMATOPOEIA

153 Anderson, Gary L. "Phonetic Symbolism and Phonological Style: A Model Grammar." *Current Trends in Stylistics*. Ed. B. B. Kachru et al. Edmonton: Linguistic Research, 1972. Pp. 163–81.

154 Barry, Peter. "The Enactment Fallacy." *Essays in Criticism* 30 (1980): 95–104.

155 Blackie, John Stuart. "On the Principle of Onomatopoeia in Language." *Horae Hellenicae*. London: Macmillan, 1874. Pp. 217–34.

156 Borroff, Marie. "Sound Symbolism as Drama in the Poetry of Wallace Stevens." *ELH* 48 (1981): 914–34.

157 Emeneau, M. B. "Onomatopoetics in the Indian Linguistic Area." *Language* 45 (1969): 274–99.

158 Epstein, Edmund L. "The Self-Reflexive Artefact: The Function of Mimesis in an Approach to a Theory of Value for Literature." *Style and Structure in Literature*. Ed. Roger Fowler. Oxford: Basil Blackwell, 1975. Pp. 40–78.

159 Firth, J. R. "Modes of Meaning." *Essays and Studies,* n.s. 4 (1951): 118–49.

160 Fónagy, Ivan. *Die Metaphern in der Phonetik: Ein Beitrag zur Entwicklungsgeschichte des wissenschaftlichen Denkens*. The Hague: Mouton, 1963. 132 pp.

161 Hill, Archibald A. "Sound-Symbolism in Lexicon and Literature." *Studies in Linguistics in Honor of George L. Trager*. Ed. M. E. Smith. The Hague: Mouton, 1972. Pp. 142–47.

162 Jespersen, Otto. "Symbolic Value of the Vowel *I*." In his *Linguistica*. Copenhagen: Levin and Munksgaard, 1933. Pp. 283–303.

163 Justice, David B. "Iconicity and Association in Phonology, Morphology, and Syntax." *Romance Philology* 33 (1980): 480–89.

❖ Kloe, Donald R. [1283].

164 Leakey, F. W. *Sound and Sense in French Poetry*. London: Bedford College, University of London, 1975.

165 Malkiel, Yakov. "From Phonosymbolism to Morphosymbolism." *The Fourth LACUS Forum, 1977*. Ed. Michel Paradis. Columbia, S.C.: Hornbeam, 1978. Pp. 469–83.

166 Mandelker, Amy. "New Research on Phonetic Symbolism: The Poetic Context." *DAI* 43, 8A (1983): 3619 (Brown).

167 Moynihan, William T. "The Auditory Correlative." *JAAC* 17 (1958): 93–102.

168 Murdy, Louise B. *Sound and Sense in Dylan Thomas's Poetry*. The Hague: Mouton, 1966. 172 pp.

169 Nodier, [Jean] Charles. *Dictionnaire raisoné des onomatopoées françaises*. 2nd ed. Paris, 1828. 403 pp. Rpt. with Introduction, "La Nature dans la voix," by Henri Meschonnic. Mauvezin: Trans-Europ-Repress, 1984. Pp. 13–104.

170 Pesot, Jurgen. *Les Onomatopées: Structure acoustique et catégories perceptuelles*. Montreal: Mémoire de l'Université de Montreal, 1973.

171 Pharies, David A. "Sound Symbolism in the Romance Languages." *DAI* 41, 1A (1980): 231 (Berkeley). 216 pp.

172 Sadler, J. D. "Onomatopoeia." *Classical Journal* 67 (1972): 174–77.

173 Weinstock, Leo I. "Onomatopoeia and Related Phenomena in Biblical Hebrew: A Survey of Certain Correlations." *DAI* 40, 6A (1979): 3268 (Pennsylvania).

174 ———. "Sound and Meaning in Biblical Hebrew." *Journal of Semitic Studies* 28 (1983): 49–62.

175 Wescott, Roger W. *Sound and Sense: Essays on Phonosemic Subjects*. Supplement to *Forum Linguisticum* 4.3 (1980). Lake Bluff, Ill.: Jupiter, 1980. 405 pp.

❖ Wilkinson, L. P. [691], chap. 3.

176 Wimsatt, W. K., Jr. "In Search of Verbal Mimesis." *Yale French Studies* 52 (1975): 229–48; rpt. in his *Day of the Leopards*. New Haven: Yale University Press, 1976. Pp. 57–73.

177 Wissemann, Heinz. *Untersuchungen zur Onomatopoiie: Die sprachpsychologischen Versuche*. Heidelberg: Carl Winter, 1954. 241 pp.

178 Wittoch, Z. "Les Onomatopées forment-elles une système dans la langue?" *Annali dell'Istituto Orientale di Napoli, Sezione Linguistica* 4 (1962): 107–47.

RHYTHM

PROSE RHYTHM

179 Aili, Hans. *The Prose Rhythm of Sallust and Livy*. Stockholm: Almqvist & Wiksell, 1979. 151 pp.

180 Baum, Paull F. *The Other Harmony of Prose: An Essay in English Prose Rhythm*. Durham: Duke University Press, 1952. 230 pp.

181 Beccaria, Gian Luigi. *Ritmo e melodia nella prosa italiana: Studi ricerche sulla prosa d'arte*. Firenze: L. S. Olschki, 1964. 334 pp.

182 Clark, Albert C. *The Cursus in Mediaeval and Vulgar Latin*. Oxford: Clarendon Press, 1910.

183   ———. *Prose Rhythm in English*. Oxford: Clarendon Press, 1913.

184   Croll, Morris W. *Style, Rhetoric, and Rhythm*. Ed. J. Max Patrick and Robert O. Evans. Princeton: Princeton University Press, 1966.

185   Denholm-Young, Noël. "The Cursus in England." *Oxford Essays in Medieval History Presented to H. E. Salter*. Oxford: Clarendon Press, 1934; rpt. in his *Collected Papers on Mediaeval Subjects*. Oxford: Basil Blackwell, 1946. Pp. 26–55.

186   Di Capua, Francesco. *Fonti ed esempi per lo studio dello "stilus curiae romanae" medioevale*. Rome: P. Maglione, 1941.

187   ———. *Il ritmo prosaico nelle lettere dei Papi nei documenti della cancellaria romana dal IV al XIV secolo*. 3 vols. Rome: Facultas theologica Pontificii athenaei seminarii Romani, 1937–46.

188   Fijn van Draat, P. *Rhythm in English Prose*. Anglistische Forschungen, vol. 29. Heidelberg: Carl Winter, 1910. 145 pp.

189   ———. "Voluptas Aurium." *Englische Studien* 48 (1915): 394–428.

190   Groot, A. Willem de. *La Prose métrique des anciens*. Paris: Société d'édition "Les Belles-Lettres," 1926. 70 pp.

191   Havet, Louis. *La Prose métrique de Symmaque et les origines métriques du cursus*. Bibliothèque de l'Ecole pratique des hautes études, fasc. 94. 1892. 112 pp.

192   Janson, Tore. *Prose Rhythm in Medieval Latin from the Ninth to the Thirteenth Century*. Stockholm: Almqvist & Wiksell, 1975.

193   Kuhn, Sherman M. "Cursus in Old English: Rhetorical Ornament or Linguistic Phenomenon?" *Speculum* 47 (1972): 188–206.

194   Laurand, Louis. "Bibliographie du *cursus*." *Revue des Études Latines* 6 (1928): 73–90; 12 (1934): 420–23.

195   Lindholm, Gudrun. *Studien zum mittellateinischen Prosarhythmus*. Stockholm: Almqvist & Wiksell, 1963. 204 pp.

❖   Meyer, Wilhelm [709], vol. 2, chaps. 7–8.

196   Poole, Reginald L. "The Ars Dictandi." *Lectures on the History of the Papal Chancery*. Cambridge: Cambridge University Press, 1915. Pp. 76–97.

197   Saintsbury, George. *A History of English Prose Rhythm*. 2nd ed. London: Macmillan, 1922; rpt. Bloomington: Indiana University Press, 1965. 482 pp.

198   Schlauch, Margaret. "The Art of Chaucer's Prose." *Chaucer and Chaucerians: Critical Studies in Middle English Literature*. Ed. D. S. Brewer. University: University of Alabama Press, 1966. Pp. 140–63.

199   ———. "Chaucer's Prose Rhythms." *PMLA* 65 (1950): 568–89.

200 Schmid, Walter. *Über die klassische Theorie und Praxis des antiken Prosarhythmus.* Hermes Einzelschriften, vol. 12. Wiesbaden: Franz Steiner, 1959. 203 pp.

201 Seckel, Dietrich. *Hölderlins Sprachrhythmus. Mit einer Einleitung über das Problem des Rhythmus und einer Bibliographie zur Rhythmus-Forschung.* Palaestra, no. 207. Leipzig: Mayer and Müller, 1937. 350 pp.

❖ Wilkinson, L. P. [691], chaps. 5-6, app. II.

202 Zielinski, Tadeusz. *Das Clauselgesetz in Ciceros Reden: Grundzüge einer oratorischen Rhythmik.* Philologus Supplementband, vol. 9. Leipzig, 1904.

203 ———. *Der constructive Rhythmus in Ciceros Reden.* Philologus Supplementband, vol. 13. Leipzig, 1914. 295 pp.

Poetic Rhythm

❖ Bely, Andrey [1354].

204 Bertinetto, P. M. *Ritmo e modelli ritmici: Analisi computazionale delle funzioni periodiche nella versificazione Dantesca.* Torino: Rosenberg and Sellier, 1973. 169 pp.

205 Bolton, T. L. "Rhythm." *American Journal of Psychology* 6 (1894): 145-238.

❖ Brogan, T. V. F. [2], chap. 5.

206 ———. "Rhythm." *Princeton Handbook* [56], pp. 238-41.

207 Cook, Albert. "Rhythm." *Prisms: Studies in Modern Literature.* Bloomington: Indiana University Press, 1967. Pp. 74-98.

208 Cureton, Richard. "Rhythm: A Multi-Level Analysis." *Style* 19 (1985): 242-57.

209 Dougherty, Adelyn. *A Study of Rhythmic Structure in the Verse of W. B. Yeats.* The Hague: Mouton, 1973. 135 pp.

210 Dürr, Walther, and Walter Gerstenberg. "Rhythmus, Metrum, Takt." *Die Musik in Geschichte und Gegenwart: Allgemeine Enzyklopädie der Musik.* Ed. Friedrich Blume. 17 vols. Kassel: Bärenreiter, 1949-86. Vol. 11, cols. 383-419.

211 Dürr, Walther, Walter Gerstenberg, and Jonathan Harvey. "Rhythm." *The New Grove Dictionary of Music and Musicians.* Ed. Stanley Sadie. 20 vols. London: Macmillan, 1981. Vol. 15, pp. 804-24.

212 Elsworth, John. "The Concept of Rhythm in Bely's Aesthetic Thought." *Andrey Bely Centenary Papers.* Ed. Boris Christa. Amsterdam: Hakkert, 1980. Pp. 68-80.

213 Groot, A. Willem de. "Der Rhythmus." *Neophilologus* 17 (1932): 81-100, 177-97, 241-65.

214 Faure, Georges. *Les Éléments du rythme poétique en anglais moderne*. The Hague: Mouton, 1970. 336 pp.

215 Fowler, Roger. "'Prose Rhythm' and Metre." In Fowler, ed. [16], pp. 82–99.

216 Fraisse, Paul. *Psychologie du rythme*. Paris: Presses Universitaire de France, 1974.

217 Frye, Northrop. *The Well-Tempered Critic*. Bloomington: Indiana University Press, 1963.

218 Georgiades, Thrasybulos. *Der griechische Rhythmus: Musik, Reigen, Vers und Sprache*. Hamburg: Marion von Schröder, 1949. 163 pp.

219 Gray, J. A. "The Form and Function of Rhythm in the Versification of *Paradise Lost*." *DAI* 28, 4A (1967): 1785 (Washington).

220 Gross, Harvey. "Prosody as Rhythmic Cognition." Introduction to his *Sound and Form in Modern Poetry* [764], pp. 10–23.

221 ———. "Toward a Phenomenology of Rhythm." Introduction to *The Structure of Verse* [20], pp. 5–17.

222 Hadley, James. "Greek Rhythm and Meter." *Essays Philological and Critical*. New York, 1873. Pp. 81–109.

223 Harding, D. W. *Words into Rhythm: English Speech Rhythm in Verse and Prose*. New York: Cambridge University Press, 1976. 166 pp.

224 Hrushovski, Benjamin. "On Free Rhythms in Modern Poetry." In Sebeok, ed. [57], pp. 173–90.

❖ Ince, Walter [1137].

225 Kibédi Varga, A. "Rythme et signification poétique." *Revue d'esthétique* 3–4 (1965): 265–86.

226 Kitto, H. D. F. "Rhythm, Metre, and Black Magic." *Classical Review* 56 (1942): 99–108.

227 Laferrière, Daniel. "The Teleology of Rhythm in Poetry: With Examples Primarily from the Russian Syllabotonic Meters." *PTL* 4 (1979): 411–50.

❖ Mazaleyrat, Jean [1100].

228 Meschonnic, Henri. *Critique du rythme: Anthropologie historique du langage*. Paris: Verdier, 1982. 720 pp.

229 Mohr, Wolfgang. "Rhythmus." In *Reallexikon,* 1st ed. [1181], vol. 3, pp. 456–75.

230 Mukařovský, Jan. "Intonation as the Basic Factor of Poetic Rhythm" (1933). *The Word and Verbal Art: Selected Essays*. Ed. and trans. John Burbank and Peter Steiner. New Haven: Yale University Press, 1977. Pp. 116–33.

231 Nist, John. "The Word-Group Cadence: Basis of English Metrics." *Linguistics* 6 (1964): 73–82.

232 Pace, George B. "The Two Domains: Meter and Rhythm." *PMLA* 76 (1961): 413–19.

233 Petersen, Eugen. "Rhythmus." *Abhandlungen der königlich Gesellschaft der Wissenschaften zu Göttingen, philologisch-historische Klasse,* n.s. 16,5 (1917): 1–104.

234 Philbrick, Charles H. "Theories of Rhythm in English and American Prosody, 1800–1950." Ph.D. diss., Brown University, 1953.

235 Richards, I. A. "Poetic Form." *Practical Criticism: A Study in Literary Judgment.* 2nd ed. New York: Harcourt, Brace, 1948. Pp. 225–34.

236 ———. "Rhythm and Metre." *Principles of Literary Criticism.* New York: Harcourt, Brace, 1925; rpt. 1948, 1961. Pp. 134–46.

237 Rosenwald, John R. "A Theory of Prosody and Rhythm." *DAI* 30, 8A (1969): 3435 (Duke).

238 Sachs, Curt. *Rhythm and Tempo: A Study in Music History.* New York: Norton, 1953 391 pp

239 Schroeder, Otto. "Rhythmus." *Hermes* 53 (1918): 324–29.

240 Seidel, Wilhelm. *Rhythmus: Eine Begriffsbestimmung.* Darmstadt: Wissenschaftliche Buchgesellschaft, 1976.

241 Seydel, Gerhard. "Rhythmica." In *Paulys Realencyclopädie* [626], ser. 2, vol. 1A, cols. 770–81.

242 Sims, D. L. "Rhythm and Meaning." *Essays in Criticism* 6 (1956): 347–52.

243 Stevenson, Charles L. "The Rhythm of English Verse." *JAAC* 28 (1970): 327–44.

244 Taig, Thomas. *Rhythm and Metre.* Cardiff: University of Wales Press, 1929. 140 pp.

245 Tarlinskaja, M. G. "Rhythm—Morphology—Syntax—Rhythm." *Style* 18 (1984): 1–26.

246 ———. "Rhythm and Meaning: 'Rhythmical Figures' in English Iambic Pentameter, Their Grammar and Their Links with Semantics." *Style* 21 (1987): 1–35.

❖ ———. *Shakespeare's Verse* [972], chap. 7.

❖ Thieme, Hugo P. [1101], chap. 9 and bibliographies, pp. 372ff., 380ff.

❖ Tynjanov, Jurij [1403].

❖ Wilkinson, L. P. [691], part 2.

247 Williams, C. F. Abdy. *The Aristoxenian Theory of Musical Rhythm.* Cambridge: Cambridge University Press, 1911.

248 Woodrow, Herbert. *A Quantitative Study of Rhythm: The Effect of Variations in Intensity, Rate, and Duration.* New York, 1909. 66 pp.

POETIC SYNTAX

249 Adams, Joseph. *Yeats and the Masks of Syntax.* New York: Columbia University Press, 1984. III pp.

250 Austin, Timothy R. *Language Crafted: A Linguistic Theory of Poetic Syntax.* Bloomington: Indiana University Press, 1984. 171 pp.

251 Baker, William E. *Syntax in English Poetry, 1870–1930.* Berkeley and Los Angeles: University of California Press, 1967.

252 Berry, Francis. *Poets' Grammar: Person, Time, and Mood in Poetry.* London: Routledge & Kegan Paul, 1958. 190 pp.

253 Bers, Victor. *Greek Poetic Syntax in the Classical Age.* New Haven: Yale University Press, 1984. 218 pp.

254 Bivens, William P., III. "Parameters of Poetic Inversion in English." *Language and Style* 12 (1979): 13–25.

❖ Brik, Osip M. "Ritm i sintaksis" [1357].

❖ Brogan [2], chap. 7.

255 Burton, Dolores M. *Shakespeare's Grammatical Style: A Computer-Assisted Analysis of "Richard II" and "Antony and Cleopatra."* Austin: University of Texas Press, 1974. 364 pp.

❖ Chatman and Levin, eds. [9], part 3.

256 Cremante, Renzo. "Nota sull'enjambement." *Lingua e Stile* 2 (1967): 377–91.

257 Cureton, Richard D. "Poetic Syntax and Aesthetic Form." *Style* 14 (1980): 318–40.

258 Davie, Donald. *Articulate Energy: An Enquiry into the Syntax of English Poetry.* 2nd ed. London: Routledge & Kegan Paul, 1976.

259 Dillon, George L. "Inversions and Deletions in English Poetry." *Language and Style* 8 (1975): 220–37.

260 Edwards, Diana C. "Clause Arrangement in Skaldic Poetry." *Arkiv* 98 (1983): 123–75.

261 Emma, Ronald D. *Milton's Grammar.* The Hague: Mouton, 1964. 164 pp.

262 Empson, William. *Seven Types of Ambiguity.* 3rd ed. London: Chatto and Windus, 1953; rpt. London: Hogarth Press, 1984.

263 Fairley, Irene. *E. E. Cummings and Ungrammar: A Study of Syntactic Deviance in His Poems.* New York: Watermill, 1975.

264 Franz, Wilhelm. *Die Sprache Shakespeares in Vers und Prosa.* Halle: Max Niemeyer, 1939. 730 pp.

265 Golomb, Harai. *Enjambement in Poetry: Language and Verse in Interaction.* Tel Aviv: Porter Institute for Poetics, Tel Aviv University, 1979. 310 pp.

266 Greenfield, Stanley B. "Ellipsis and Meaning in Poetry." *Texas Studies in Literature and Language* 13 (1971): 137–47.

267 ———. "Grammar and Meaning in Poetry." *PMLA* 82 (1967): 377–87.

❖ Havens, R. D. [947].

268 Hollander, John. " 'Sense Variously Drawn Out': Some Observations on English Enjambment." In Hollander [22], pp. 91–116.

269 Jakobson, Roman. "Poetry of Grammar and Grammar of Poetry." *Lingua* 21 (1968): 597–609; rpt. in his *Poetry of Grammar and Grammar of Poetry.* Vol. 3 of the *Selected Writings.* Ed. Stephen Rudy. The Hague: Mouton, 1981. Pp. 87–97.

270 Jones, Lawrence G. "Grammatical Patterns in English and Russian Verse." In *To Honor Roman Jakobson* [99], vol. 2, pp. 1015–45.

271 Kenner, Hugh. "Some Post-Symbolist Structures." *Literary Theory and Structure: Essays in Honor of W. K. Wimsatt.* Ed. Martin Price. New Haven: Yale University Press, 1973. Pp. 379–93.

272 Kerkhof, J. *Studies in the Language of Geoffrey Chaucer.* 2nd ed., rev. Leiden, E. J. Brill, 1982. 251 pp.

273 Kirk, G. S. "Studies in Some Technical Aspects of Homeric Style, II: Verse-structure and Sentence-structure in Homer." *Yale Classical Studies* 20 (1966): 73–152.

274 Klee, Frederich. *Das Enjambement bei Chaucer.* Halle, 1913. 70 pp.

275 Laferrière, Daniel. "Automorphic Structures in the Poem's Grammatical Space." *Semiotica* 10 (1974): 333–50; rpt. in his *Sign and Subject.* Lisse: Peter de Ridder, 1978. Pp. 16–31.

276 Langworthy, Charles A. "Verse-Sentence Patterns in English Poetry." *Philological Quarterly* 7 (1928): 283–98.

277 Lawler, Justus G. "Commerce." *Celestial Pantomime.* New Haven: Yale University Press, 1979. Pp. 73–103.

278 Levin, Samuel R. "Deviation—Statistical and Determinate—in Poetic Language." *Lingua* 12 (1963): 276–90.

279 Levý, Jiří. "Rhythmical Ambivalence in the Poetry of T. S. Eliot." *Anglia* 77 (1959): 54–64.

280 Mitchell, Bruce. *Old English Syntax*. 2 vols. Oxford: Clarendon Press, 1985. 820 + 1080 pp.

281 Mitchell, Roger. "Toward a System of Grammatical Scansion." *Language and Style* 3 (1970): 3–28.

❖   Morier, Henri [1104].

282 Parry, Milman. "The Distinctive Character of Enjambement in Homeric Verse." In Parry [315], pp. 251–65.

283 Redin, Mats. *Word-Order in English Verse from Pope to Sassoon*. Uppsala: Almqvist & Wiksell, 1925. 225 pp.

284 Robinson, Fred C. *"Beowulf" and the Appositive Style*. Knoxville: University of Tennessee Press, 1985.

285 Rogers, J. P. W. "Pope and the Syntax of Satire." *Literary English Since Shakespeare*. Ed. George Watson. London: Oxford University Press, 1970. Pp. 236–65.

286 Strzetelski, Jerzy. *The English Sonnet: Syntax and Style*. Cracow: Jagiell University, 1970. 146 pp.

287 Taranovsky, Kiril. "Some Problems of Enjambement in Slavic and Western European Verse." *International Journal of Slavic Linguistics and Poetics,* no. 7 (1963): 80–87.

288 Wexler, P. J. "Distich and Sentence in Corneille and Racine." In Fowler, ed. [16], pp. 100–117.

289 ———. "On the Grammetrics of the Classical Alexandrine." *Cahiers de Lexicologie* 4 (1964): 61–72.

❖   Wilkinson, L. P. [691], chaps. 7–8.

THE PERFORMANCE OF POETRY

DELIVERY

❖   Brogan [2], chap. 10.

290 Chatman, Seymour. "Linguistic Style, Literary Style, and Performance." *Monograph Series on Language and Linguistics* 13 (1962): 73–81.

291 Crosby, Ruth. "Chaucer and the Custom of Oral Delivery." *Speculum* 13 (1938): 413–32.

292 ———. "Oral Delivery in the Middle Ages." *Speculum* 11 (1936): 88–110.

293 Forrest, W. C. "The Poem as a Summons to Performance." *British Journal of Aesthetics* 9 (1969): 298–305.

294 Hardison, O. B., Jr. "Speaking the Speech." *Shakespeare Quarterly* 34 (1983): 133–46.

295 Hein, Hilde. "Performance as an Aesthetic Category." *Journal of Aesthetics and Art Criticism* 28 (1970): 381–86.

296 Levin, Samuel R. "Suprasegmentals and the Performance of Poetry." *Quarterly Journal of Speech* 48 (1962): 366–72.

297 Loesch, Katharine T. "Empirical Studies in Oral Interpretation: The Text." *Western Speech* 38 (1969): 250–68.

298 ———. "Literary Ambiguity and Oral Performance." *Quarterly Journal of Speech* 51 (1965): 258–67.

299 Quinn, K. "The Poet and His Audience in the Augustan Age." *Aufstieg und Niedergang der römischen Welt*. Ed. W. Haase. 2 vols. Berlin: De Gruyter, 1982. Vol. 2, pp. 75–180.

Language Poetry

300 Andrews, Bruce, and Charles Bernstein, eds. *The L=A=N=G=U=A=G=E Book*. Carbondale: Southern Illinois University Press, 1984.

301 Kostelanetz, Richard, ed. *The Old Poetries and the New*. Ann Arbor: University of Michigan Press, 1981. 316 pp.

302 ———. *Text-Sound Texts*. New York: William Morrow, 1980. 441 pp.

303 Perloff, Marjorie. "The Word as Such: L=A=N=G=U=A=G=E Poetry in the Eighties." In Perloff [550], pp. 215–38.

304 Vincent, Stephen, and Ellen Zweig, eds. *The Poetry Reading: A Contemporary Compendium of Language and Performance*. San Francisco: Momos, 1981. 351 pp.

305 Zweig, Ellen M. "Performance Poetry: Critical Approaches to Contemporary Intermedia." *DAI* 41, 2A (1980): 661 (Michigan).

Oral Tradition

306 Finnegan, Ruth. *Oral Poetry: Its nature, significance, and social context*. Cambridge: Cambridge University Press, 1977. 299 pp.

❖ ———. *Oral Poetry in Africa* [1486].

307 Foley, John Miles, ed. *Oral Formulaic Theory and Research: An Introduction and Bibliography*. New York: Garland, 1985. 718 pp.

Surveys 1,800 items.

308 Hainsworth, J. B. *The Flexibility of the Homeric Formula.* Oxford: Clarendon Press, 1968. 147 pp.

309 Hoekstra, A. *Homeric Modifications of Formulaic Prototypes: Studies in the Development of Greek Epic Diction.* Amsterdam: North-Holland, 1965.

310 Janko, Richard. *Homer, Hesiod, and the Hymns: Diachronic Developments in Epic Diction.* Cambridge: Cambridge University Press, 1982. 322 pp.

311 Kirk, G. S. *Homer and the Oral Tradition.* Cambridge: Cambridge University Press, 1976. 222 pp.

312 Lord, Albert B. *The Singer of Tales.* Cambridge, Mass.: Harvard University Press, 1960. 307 pp.

313 Niles, John D. "Formula and Formulaic System in *Beowulf.*" *Oral Traditional Literature: A Festschrift for Albert Bates Lord.* Ed. John Miles Foley. Columbus, Ohio: Slavica, 1981. Pp. 394–415.

314 Opland, Jeff. *Anglo-Saxon Oral Poetry: A Study of the Traditions.* New Haven: Yale University Press, 1980. 289 pp.

315 Parry, Milman. *The Making of Homeric Verse: The Collected Papers of Milman Parry.* Ed. Adam Parry. Oxford: Clarendon Press, 1971. 483 pp.

316 Peabody, Berkley. *The Winged Word: A Study in the Technique of Ancient Greek Oral Composition as Seen Principally through Hesiod's "Works and Days."* Albany: State University of New York Press, 1975. 562 pp.

317 Quinn, William, and Audley S. Hall. *Jongleur: A Modified Theory of Oral Improvisation and Its Effects on the Performance and Transmission of Middle English Romance.* Washington, D.C.: University Press of America, 1982. 423 pp.

318 Stotz, Benjamin A., and R. S. Shannon, eds. *Oral Literature and the Formula.* Ann Arbor: Center for the Coordination of Ancient and Modern Studies, University of Michigan, 1976.

319 Toelken, J. Barre. "An Oral Canon for the Child Ballads: Construction and Application." *Journal of the Folklore Institute* 4 (1967): 75–101.

320 Watts, Ann Chalmers. *The Lyre and the Harp: A Comparative Reconsideration of Oral Tradition in Homer and Old English Epic Poetry.* New Haven: Yale University Press, 1969. 279 pp.

321 Webber, Ruth D. *Formulistic Diction in the Spanish Ballad.* University of California Publications in Modern Philology, vol. 34, no. 2. Berkeley and Los Angeles: University of California Press, 1951. Pp. 175–277.

322 Whallon, William. *Formula, Character, and Context: Studies in Homeric, Old English, and Old Testament Poetry.* Cambridge, Mass.: Harvard University Press, 1969. 225 pp.

323 Zwettler, Michael. *The Oral Tradition in Classical Arabic Poetry: Its Character and Implication.* Columbus: Ohio State University Press, 1978. 310 pp.

STANZA FORMS

GENERAL STUDIES

Also note the specialized stanza indexes listed in chapters 16–20.

❖ Bec, Pierre [489].

❖ Brogan, T. V. F. [2], chap. 8.

324 Cohen, Helen L. *Lyric Forms from France: Their History and Their Use.* New York: Harcourt, Brace, 1922.

325 Dacey, Philip, and David Jauss, eds. "Introduction." *Strong Measures: Contemporary American Poetry in Traditional Forms.* New York: Harper & Row, 1985. 492 pp.

326 Gennrich, Friedrich, ed. *Rondeaux, Virelais, und Balladen aus dem Ende des XII, des XIII und ersten Drittel des XIV Jahrhunderts.* 3 vols. Dresden, 1921, and Göttingen, 1927: Gesellschaft für romanische Literatur; Frankfurt: Langen bei Frankfurt, 1963.

327 Gosse, Edmund. "A Plea for Certain Exotic Forms of Verse." *Cornhill Magazine* 36 (1877): 53–71.

328 Häublein, Ernst. *The Stanza.* Critical Idiom Series, vol. 38. London: Methuen, 1978. 125 pp.

❖ Le Gentil, Pierre [1285].

329 Omans, G. A. "Medieval French Poetic Forms in Victorian Poetry." *DAI* 24, 3A (1963): 1173 (Minnesota).

❖ Scott, Clive [1162], chaps. 5–6.

330 Stratton, Clarence. "The Italian Lyrics of Sidney's *Arcadia*." *Sewanee Review* 25 (1917): 305–26.

331 Suppan, Wolfgang. "Strophe." In *Reallexikon,* 2nd ed. [1182], vol. 4, pp. 245–56.

332 Turco, Lewis. *The New Book of Forms: A Handbook of Poetics.* Hanover, N.H.: University Press of New England, 1986. 280 pp.

333 White, J. Gleeson. *Ballades and rondeaus, chants royal, sestinas, villanelles, &., selected, with a chapter on the various forms.* London, 1887; New York, 1888. 296 pp.

334 Wilkins, Nigel. *One Hundred Ballades, Rondeaux and Virelais from the Late Middle Ages*. Cambridge: Cambridge University Press, 1969.

335 Williams, Miller. *Patterns of Poetry: An Encyclopedia of Forms*. Baton Rouge: Louisiana State University Press, 1986. 203 pp.

ALBA, AUBE

336 Hatto, Arthur T., ed. *Eos: An Enquiry into the Theme of Lovers' Meetings and Partings at Dawn in Poetry.* The Hague: Mouton, 1965.

BALLADE

337 Cohen, Helen L. *The Ballade*. New York: Columbia University Press, 1915. 397 pp.

❖ Cohen, Helen L. [324].

338 Friedman, Albert B. "The Late Medieval Ballade and the Origin of Broadside Balladry." *Medium Ævum* 27 (1958): 95–110.

339 Hecq, Gaëtan M. *La Ballade et ses derivées*. Brussels, 1891.

❖ Kastner, L. E. [1106].

340 Reaney, Gilbert. "Concerning the Origins of the Rondeau, Virelai, and Ballade." *Musica Disciplina* 6 (1952): 155–66.

341 ———. "The Development of the Rondeau, Virelai, and Ballade Forms from Adam de la Hale to Guillaume de Machaut." *Festschrift für Karl Fellerer.* Ed. Heinrich Hues. Rogensburg, 1962. Pp. 421–27.

BOB AND WHEEL

342 Kirkpatrick, Hugh. "The Bob-Wheel and Allied Stanzas in Middle English and Middle Scots Poetry." *DAI* 37, 6A (1976): 3608 (North Texas State).

343 Stanley, E. G. "The Use of Bob-Lines in *Sir Thopas.*" *Neuphilologische Mitteilungen* 73 (1972): 417–26.

Including a catalogue of all other attested examples in Middle English.

344 Turville-Petre, Thorlac. " 'Summer Sunday,' 'De Tribus Regibus Mortuis' and 'The Awntyrs off Arthure': Three Poems in the Thirteen-Line Stanza." *Review of English Studies* 25 (1974): 1–14.

CANZONE

❖ Barber, Joseph A. [1303–4].

345 Gáldi, Ladislas. "Les Origines provençales de la métrique des 'canzoni' de Pétrarque." *Actes Romanes* 74 (1966): 783–90.

346 Gonfroy, Gérard. "Le Reflet de la canso dans *De vulgari eloquentia* et dans les *Leys d'amors.*" *Cahiers de Civilisation Médiévale* 25 (1982): 187–96.

347 Hunt, Clay. *"Lycidas" and the Italian Critics.* New Haven: Yale University Press, 1979. 196 pp.

348 Köhler, Erich. " 'Vers' und Kanzone." In *GRLM* [1103], vol. 2, *Les Genres Lyriques*, part 1, no. 3 (1987): 45–176.

❖ Memmo, Francesco Paolo [1299], s.v. "Canzone," "Coblas," et seq.

349 Mumford, Ivy L. "The Canzone in Sixteenth-Century English Verse." *English Miscellany* 11 (1960): 21–32

❖ Pazzaglia, Mario [1328].

CAROL

350 Greene, Richard Leighton, ed. *The Early English Carols.* 2nd ed., rev. Oxford: Clarendon Press, 1977. 517 pp.

351 Robbins, Rossell Hope. "The Burden in Carols." *MLN* 57 (1942): 16–22.

352 Schöpf, Manfred. "Zur Strophenform einiger Carols." *Anglia* 87 (1969): 394–97.

DESCORT

353 Jeanroy, Alfred, Louis Brandin, and Pierre Aubry, eds. "La Versification dans les lais et descorts." *Lais et descorts français du XIIIe siècle: Texte et musique.* Paris: H. Welter, 1901. Pp. v–x.

354 Köhler, Erich. "Descort und lai." In *GRLM* [1103], vol. 2, *Les Genres Lyriques*, part 4, no. 1 (1980): 1–8.

355 Lang, Henry R. "The *Descort* in Old Portuguese and Spanish Poetry." *Beiträge zur romanischen Philologie: Festgabe für Gustav Gröber.* Halle, 1899. Pp. 484–506.

❖ Maillard, Jean. *Evolution et esthétique du lai lyrique* [363], p. 119ff.

356 ———. "Problèmes musicaux et littéraires du descort." *Mélanges de linguistique et de littérature romanes à la mémoire d'István Frank.* Saarbrück: Universität des Saarlandes, 1957. Pp. 388–409.

357 Marshall, J. H. "The Isostrophic *descort* in the Poetry of the Troubadours." *Romance Philology* 35 (1981): 130–57.

HAIKU AND TANKA

358 Etiemble, René. "Dialectique du vers libre et du haiku." *Revue de Littérature Comparée* 51 (1977): 212–22.

359 ———. "Sur une bibliographie du *haiku* dans les langues européennes." *Comparative Literature Studies* 11 (1974): 1–20.

360 Figgins, Ross. "A Basic Bibliography of Haiku in English." *Bulletin of Bibliography* 36 (1979): 45–49.

❖ Kodama, Sanehide [1481].

❖ Miner, Earl, Hiroko Odagiri, and Robert E. Morrell [1484].

361 Record, Alison K. "Haiku Genre: The Nature and Origin of English Haiku." *DAI* 44, 12A (1984): 3679 (Indiana).

LAI

❖ Jeanroy, Alfred, Louis Brandin, and Pierre Aubry, eds. [353].

❖ Köhler, Erich [354].

362 Le Mée, Katherine W. *A Metrical Study of Five Lais of Marie de France.* The Hague: Mouton, 1978. 202 pp.

363 Maillard, Jean. *Evolution et esthétique du lai lyrique: Des Origines à la fin du XIVe siècle.* Paris: Centre de Documentation Universitaire, 1963. 395 pp.

364 ———. "Problèmes musicaux et littéraires du lai." *Quadrivium* 2 (1957): 32–44.

365 Reaney, Gilbert. "Concerning the Origins of the Medieval Lai." *Music and Letters* 39 (1958): 343–46.

366 Spanke, Hans. "Sequenz und Lai." *Studi Medievali,* n.s. 11 (1938): 12–68.

367 Wolf, Ferdinand. *Über die Lais, Sequenzen, und Leiche. Ein Beitrag zur Geschichte der rythmischen Formen und Singweisen der Volkslieder und der volksmässigen Kirchen- und Kunstliederim Mittelalter.* Heidelberg, 1841.

LIMERICK

368 Belknap, George N. "History of the Limerick." *PBSA* 75 (1981): 1–32.

369 Legman, Gershon, ed. *The Limerick: 1700 Examples, with notes, variants, and index*. San Francisco: Greenleaf Classics [c. 1969].

NIBELUNGENSTROPHE

370 Habermann, Paul. "Nibelungenstrophe." *Reallexikon* [1181], vol. 2, pp. 496–500.

371 Henning, Rudolf. "Metrik." *Nibelungenstudien*. Strassburg, 1883. Pp. 253–92.

❖ Heusler, Andreas [1185].

372 Kulsdom, G. J. H. *Die Strophenschlüsse im Nibelungenlied: Ein Versuch*. Amsterdam: Rodopi, 1979. 260 pp.

373 Panzer, Friedrich. *Das Nibelungenlied*. Stuttgart: W. Kohlhammer, 1955.

❖ Pretzel, Ulrich, with supp. by Helmuth Thomas [1187].

374 Rompelman, Tom. "Zur Strophik des Nibelungenlieds." *Altgermanische Beiträge Jan van Dam*. Ed. Friedrich Maurer and Cola Minis. Amsterdam: Rodopi, 1977. Pp. 33–59.

375 Simrock, K. *Die Nibelungenstrophe und ihre Ursprung*. Bonn, 1858.

376 Stutz, Elfriede. "Das Nibelungenzeile: Dauer und Wandel." *Philologische Studien für Richard Kienast*. Ed. Ute Schwab and Elfriede Stutz. Heidelberg: Carl Winter, 1978. Pp. 96–130.

ODE

377 Fry, Paul H. "Ode." *Princeton Handbook* [56], pp. 171–73.

378 Habermann, Paul. "Antike Versmasse und Strophen- (Oden-)formen im Deutschen," *Reallexikon*, 1st ed. [1181], vol. 1, pp. 70–84.

379 Janik, Dieter. *Geschichte der Ode und der Stances von Ronsard bis Boileau*. Bad Hamburg: Gehlen, 1968. 242 pp.

380 Jump, John D. "Lax and Lawless Versification." *The Ode*. Critical Idiom Series, vol. 30. London: Methuen, 1974. Pp. 14–23.

381 Maddison, Carl. *Apollo and the Nine: A History of the Ode*. Baltimore: Johns Hopkins Press, 1960. 427 pp.

382 Schlüter, Kurt. *Die englische Ode: Studien zu ihrer Entwicklung unter dem Einfluss der antiken Hymne*. Bonn: Bouvier, 1964. 335 pp.

383 Shafer, Robert. *The English Ode to 1660: An Essay in Literary History*. New York, 1918; rpt. New York: Gordian, 1966.

384 Shuster, George N. *The English Ode from Milton to Keats*. New York: Columbia University Press, 1940.

385 Teich, Nathaniel. "The Ode in English Literary History: Transformations from the Mid-Eighteenth to the Early Nineteenth Century." *Papers in Language and Literature* 21 (1985): 88–108.

386 Wiegand, Julius, and Werner Kohlschmidt. "Ode." *Reallexikon*, 2nd ed. [1182], vol. 2, pp. 709–17.

OTTAVA RIMA

387 Beum, Robert. "Yeats's Octaves." In Beum [784], pp. 120–31.

❖ Elwert, W. Theodor [1316].

388 Limentani, Alberto. "Storia e struttura dell'ottava rima." *Lettere Italiane* 13 (1961): 20–77.

389 Moran, Ronald. "The Octaves of E. A. Robinson." *Colby Library Quarterly*, ser. 8, no. 7 (1969): 363–70.

390 Roncaglia, Aurelio. "Per la storia dell'ottava rima." *Cultura Neolatina* 25 (1965): 5–14.

PANTOUM

391 Brewster, Paul G. "Metrical, Stanzaic and Stylistic Resemblances between Malayan and Western Poetry." *Revue de Littérature Comparée* 32 (1958): 214–22.

392 Etiemble, René. "Du 'Pantun' malais au 'pantoum' à la française." *Zagadnienia Rodzajów Literackich* 22,2 (1979): 21–31.

RHYME ROYAL

393 Cowling, G. H. "A Note on Chaucer's Stanza." *Review of English Studies* 2 (1926): 311–17.

394 Maynard, Theodore. *The Connection between the Ballade, Chaucer's Modification of It, Rime Royal, and the Spenserian Stanza*. Washington, D.C.: Catholic University of America Press, 1934. 140 pp.

395 Stevens, Martin. "The Royal Stanza in Early English Literature." *PMLA* 94 (1979): 62–76.

RONDEAU

396 Boogaard, Nico H. J. van den, ed. *Rondeaux et refrains du XIIe siècle au début du XIVe.* Bibliothèque française et romane, Strasbourg, ser. D, no. 3. Paris: Klinksieck, 1969.

397 Cocking, J. M. "The Invention of the Rondel." *French Studies* 5 (1951): 49–55.

❖ Cohen, Helen L. [324].

398 Françon, Marcel. "Rondeaux Tercets." *Speculum* 24 (1949): 88–92.

399 ———. "Wyatt et le Rondeau." *Renaissance Quarterly* 24 (1971): 340–43.

400 Gennrich, Friedrich. *Das altfranzösische Rondeau und Virelai im 12. und 13. Jahrhunderts.* Frankfurt: Langen bei Frankfurt, 1963.

401 ———. "Deutsche Rondeaux." *Beiträge zur Geschichte der Deutsche Sprache und Literatur* 72 (1950): 130–41.

402 Gennrich, Friedrich, G. Reaney, and Hans Engel. "Rondeau—Rondo." In *MGG* [210], vol. 11, cols. 867–83.

❖ Gennrich, Friedrich, ed. [326].

❖ Kastner, L. E. [1106].

403 Rat, Maurice. "Rondel et rondeau." *Vie et Langage* 14 (1965): 267–75.

❖ Reaney, Gilbert [340–41].

404 Scott, Clive. "The Revival of the Rondel in France and England, 1860–1920: A Comparative Study." *Revue de Littérature Comparée* 213 (1980): 32–46.

❖ Scott, Clive [1162], pp. 164–71.

405 Spanke, Hans. "Das lateinische Rondeau." *Zeitschrift für Französische Sprache und Literatur* 53 (1929–30): 113–48.

❖ Thieme, Hugo P. [1101], p. 380.

Lists ten French works, 1364–1897.

406 Tierney, Frank M. "The Causes of the Revival of the Rondeau in Nineteenth-Century England." *Revue de l'Université d'Ottawa* 43 (1973): 95–113.

407 ———. "The Development of the Rondeau in English from Its Origin in the Middle Ages to Its Revival in the Years following 1860." *Revue de l'Université d'Ottawa* 41 (1971): 25–46.

408 Wilkins, Nigel. "Rondeau." In *New Grove* [211], vol. 16, pp. 166–70.

SAPPHIC

409 Brocks, Emil. *Die Sapphische Strophe*. Marienwerder, 1890. 37 pp.

410 Hjärne, Erland. "Den sapfiska strofen i svensk verskonst." *Sprak och Stil* 13 (1913): 275–317.

411 Kenner, Hugh. "The Muse in Tatters." *Agenda* 6 (1968): 43–61.

412 Needler, G. H. "The Metrical Ancestry." *The Lone Shieling: Origin and Authorship of the Blackwood "Canadian Boat-Song."* Toronto: University of Toronto Press, 1941. Pp. 7–51.

413 Page, D. L. "Appendix on Metres." *Sappho and Alcaeus*. Oxford: Clarendon Press, 1955; rpt. 1979. Pp. 318–26.

414 Paulin, Roger. "Six Sapphic Odes, 1753–1934." *Seminar: A Journal of Germanic Studies* 10 (1974): 181–98.

415 Rüdiger, Horst. "Das sappische Versmass in der deutschen Literatur." *Zeitschrift für Deutsche Philologie* 58 (1933): 140–64.

416 Schäfer, Eckart. *Deutscher Horaz: Die Nachwirkung des Horaz in der neulateinischen Dichtung Deutschlands*. Wiesbaden: Steiner, 1976. 280 pp.

417 Stotz, Peter. *Sonderformen der sappischen Dichtung: Ein Beitrag zur Erforschung der sappischen Dichtung des lateinischen Mittelalters*. Munich: Wilhelm Fink, 1982. 535 pp.

418 Weber, Edith. "Prosodie verbale et prosodie musicale: La Strophe sapphique au Moyen Age et à la Renaissance." *Le Moyen Français* 5 (1979): 159–92.

SEGUIDILLA

419 Clarke, Dorothy Clotelle. "The Early Seguidilla." *Hispanic Review* 12 (1944): 211–22.

420 Hanssen, Federico. "La seguidilla." *Anales de la Universidad de Chile* 125 (1909): 697–796.

❖ Navarro Tomás, Tomás [1290].

SESTINA

❖ Baldelli, Ignazio [1302].

421 Battaglia, Salvatore. *La rime "petrose" e la sestina: Arnaldo Danielo, Dante, Petrarca*. Naples: Liguorini, 1964. 139 pp.

422 Cummins, Paul. "The Sestina in the Twentieth Century." *Concerning Poetry* 11 (1978): 15–23.

❖ Elwert, W. Theodor [1316].

423 Fiedler, Leslie A. " 'Green Thoughts in a Green Shade': Thoughts on the Stony Sestina of Dante Alighieri." *Kenyon Review* 18 (1956): 238–62.

424 Gramont, Ferdinand de. *Sextines, précédés de l'histoire de la sextine dans les langues dérivées du latin*. Paris, 1872. 68 pp.

425 Jeanroy, Alfred. "La 'sestina doppia' de Dante et les origines de la sextine." *Romania* 42 (1912): 481–89.

426 Jernigan, John C. "The Sestina in Provence, Italy, France, and England (1180–1600)." *DAI* 31, 12A (1971): 6554 (Indiana).

427 Nims, John Frederick. "The Sestina." *A Local Habitation: Essays on Poetry*. Ann Arbor: University of Michigan Press, 1985. Pp. 269–306.

428 Riesz, János. *Die Sestine: Ihre Stellung in der literarischen Kritik und ihre Geschichte als lyrisches Genus*. Munich: Wilhelm Fink, 1971. 328 pp.

Includes bibliography.

429 Shapiro, Marianne. *Hieroglyph of Time: The Petrarchan Sestina*. Minneapolis: University of Minnesota Press, 1980. 254 pp.

SONNET

430 Biadene, Leandro. *Morfologia del sonetto nei secoli XIII e XIV*. Rome: E. Löscher, 1889; rpt. Florence: Lettere, 1977. 234 pp.

431 Booth, Stephen. *An Essay on Shakespeare's Sonnets*. New Haven: Yale University Press, 1969.

432 Bullock, Walter L. "The Genesis of the English Sonnet Form." *PMLA* 38 (1923): 729–44.

433 Donow, Herbert S. *The Sonnet in England and America: A Bibliography of Criticism*. Westport, Conn.: Greenwood, 1982. 477 pp.

434 Fechner, Jörg Ulrich, ed. *Das deutsche Sonett: Dichtungen, Gattungspoetik, Dokumente*. Munich: Wilhelm Fink, 1969. 456 pp.

435 Hornsby, Sam, and James R. Bennett. "The Sonnet: An Annotated Bibliography from 1940 to the Present." *Style* 13 (1979): 162–77.

436 Jost, François. "The Sonnet in Its European Context." *Introduction to Comparative Literature*. Indianapolis: Bobbs-Merrill, 1974. Pp. 151–72.

❖ Kastner, L. E. [1106].

437 Kimmich, Flora. "Sonnets before Opitz: The Evolution of a Form." *German Quarterly* 49 (1976): 456–71.

438 Kircher, Hartmut, ed. *Deutsche Sonette*. Stuttgart: Reclam, 1979. 539 pp.

439 Lever, J. W. *The Elizabethan Love Sonnet*. 2nd. ed. London: Methuen, 1965.

440 Levý, Jiří. "The Development of Rhyme-Scheme and of Syntactic Pattern in
441 the English Renaissance Sonnet" and "On the Relations of Language and
Stanza Pattern in the English Sonnet." Both rpt. in his *Paralipomena* [1382],
pp. 22–42, 43–61.

Includes bibliography.

442 Lopez Bueno, Begoña, ed. *Sonetos y madrigales completos*. Madrid: Cätedra,
1981. 345 pp.

443 Mönch, Walter. *Das Sonett: Gestalt und Geschichte*. Heidelberg: F. H. Kerle,
1955. 341 pp.

❖ Morier, Henri [1104].

444 Núñez Mata, Efrén. *Historia y origen del soneto*. Mexico: Ediciones Botas,
1967. 298 pp.

445 Oliphant, E. H. C. "Sonnet Structure: An Analysis." *Philological Quarterly*
11 (1932): 135–48.

446 Olmsted, Everett W. *The Sonnet in French Literature and the Development of
the Sonnet Form*. Ithaca, 1897.

447 Oppenheimer, Paul. "The Origin of the Sonnet." *Comparative Literature* 34
(1982): 289–304.

448 Prince, F. T. "The Sonnet from Wyatt to Shakespeare." *Elizabethan Poetry*.
Ed. John Russell Brown and Bernard Harris. London: Edward Arnold, 1960.
Pp. 11–29.

449 Rivers, Elias L. "Certain Formal Characteristics of the Primitive Love Sonnet." *Speculum* 33 (1958): 42–55.

450 Romanov, Boris. "Russkij sonet." *Russkij sonet: Sonety russkix poe'tov XVIII–
nachala XX veka*. Moscow: Sovetska, 1983. Pp. 3–24.

❖ Schipper, Jakob [769].

451 Schlütter, Hans-Jürgen. *Sonett*. Stuttgart: Metzler, 1979.

452 Scott, Clive. "The Limits of the Sonnet: Towards a Proper Contemporary
Approach." *Revue de Littérature Comparée* 50 (1976): 237–50.

❖ Scott, Clive [1162], pp. 171–81.

453 Scott, David H. *Sonnet Theory and Practice in Nineteenth-Century France: Sonnets on the Sonnet*. Hull: University of Hull, 1977.

❖ Strzetelski, Jerzy [286].

❖ Thieme, Hugo P. [1101], pp. 381–82.

Lists seventeen French works, 1548–1903.

454 Weeks, L. T. "The Order of Rhymes of the English Sonnet." *MLN* 25
(1910): 176–80, 231.

455 Welti, Heinrich. *Geschichte des Sonettes in der deutschen Dichtung.* Leipzig, 1884. 255 pp.

456 Wilkins, Ernest Hatch. *The Invention of the Sonnet and Other Studies in Italian Literature.* Rome: Edizioni di storia e letteratura, 1959. 354 pp.

SPENSERIAN

457 Alpers, Paul J. *The Poetry of "The Faerie Queene."* Princeton: Princeton University Press, 1967.

458 Corse, L. B. "The Influence of Lyric Poetry and Music on Prosodic Technique in the Spenserian Stanza." *DAI* 33, 8A (1973): 4404 (North Texas State).

❖ Empson, William [262].

❖ Maynard, Theodore [394].

459 Morton, Edward P. "The Spenserian before 1700." *Modern Philology* 4 (1907): 639–54.

460 ———. "The Spenserian Stanza in the Eighteenth Century." *Modern Philology* 10 (1913): 365–91.

461 Pope, Emma F. "The Critical Background of the Spenserian Stanza." *Modern Philology* 24 (1926): 31–53.

462 Reschke, Hedwig. *Die Spenserstanze bei den Spensernachahmern des neunzehnten Jahrhunderts.* Heidelberg: Carl Winter, 1918. 198 pp.

TAIL RHYME

463 Damico, Helen. "Sources of Stanza Forms Used by Burns." *Studies in Scottish Literature* 12 (1975): 207–19.

464 Dürmüller, Urs. *Narrative Possibilities of the Tail-Rime Romances.* Bern: Francke, 1975. 245 pp.

465 Gaylord, Alan T. "Chaucer's Dainty 'Dogerel': The 'Elvyssh' Prosody of *Sir Thopas*." *Studies in the Age of Chaucer* 1 (1979): 83–104.

466 Mitchell, Jerome. "Wordsworth's Tail-Rhyme 'Lucy' Poem." *Studies in Medieval Culture* 4 (1974): 561–68.

467 Strong, Caroline. "History and Relations of the Tail-Rhyme Strophe in Latin, French, and English." *PMLA* 22 (1907): 371–420.

468 Trounce, A. McI. "The English Tail-Rhyme Romances." *Medium Ævum* 1 (1932): 87–108, 168–82; 2 (1933): 34–57, 189–98; 3 (1934): 30–50.

TERZA RIMA

❖ Baldelli, Ignazio [1302].

469 Bernheim, Roger. *Die Terzine in der deutschen Dichtung von Goethe bis Hof-mannsthal.* Düsseldorf: Zentral-Verlag für Dissertationen Triltsch, 1954. 140 pp.

470 Binyon, Laurence. "Terza Rima in English Poetry." *English* 3 (1940): 113–17.

❖ Boyde, Patrick [1310–11].

471 Freccero, John. "The Significance of Terza Rima." *Dante, Petrarch, Boccaccio: Studies in the Trecento.* Ed. Aldo S. Bernardo and A. L. Pellegrini. Bingham-ton, N.Y.: Medieval and Renaissance Text Society, 1983. Pp. 3–17.

472 Fubini, M. "La Terzina della *Commedia.*" *Deutsches Dante Jahrbuch* 43 (1965): 58–89.

473 Kastner, L. E. "History of the Terza Rima in France." *Zeitschrift für französische Sprache und Literatur* 26 (1904): 241–53.

474 Schuchardt, Hugo E. M. *Ritornell und Terzine.* Halle, 1875. 146 pp.

475 Tatlock, J. S. P. "Dante's *Terza Rima.*" *PMLA* 51 (1936): 895–903.

476 Wain, John. "Terza Rima: A Foot Note on English Prosody." *Rivista di Letterature Moderne* 1 (1950): 44–48.

TRIOLET

477 Marcotte, Paul J. "An Introduction to the Triolet." *Inscape* 5 (1966): 18–31.

478 ———. "More Late Victorian Triolet Makers." *Inscape* 6,2 (1968): 1–18.

479 ———. "A Trio of Triolet Turners." *Inscape* 6,1 (1968): 1–19.

❖ Morier, Henri [1104].

480 Scott, Clive. "The Nineteenth-Century Triolet: French and English Explo-rations of a Form." *Orbis Litterarum* 35 (1980): 357–72

481 Spitzer, Leo. "Triolet." *Romanic Review* 39 (1948): 146–55.

VILLANELLE

482 Jason, Philip K. "Modern Versions of the Villanelle." *College Literature* 7 (1980): 136–45.

❖ Kastner, L. E. [1106].

483 McFarland, Ronald E. "The Contemporary Villanelle." *Modern Poetry Studies* 11 (1982): 113–27.

484 ———. "Victorian Villanelles." *Victorian Poetry* 20 (1982): 125–38.

❖ Morier, Henri. [1104].

❖ Scott, Clive [1162], pp. 157–64.

VIRELAI

485 Françon, Marcel. "On the Nature of the Virelai." *Symposium* 9 (1955): 348–52.

486 Gennrich, Friedrich, and Gilbert Reaney. "Virelai." In *MGG* [210], vol. 13, cols. 1802–7.

❖ Kastner, L. E. [1106].

487 Le Gentil, Pierre. *Le Virelai et le villancico: Le Problème des origines arabes.* Madrid: Les Belles Lettres, 1954.

❖ Morier, Henri [1104].

❖ Reaney, Gilbert [340–41].

488 Wilkins, Nigel. "Virelai." In *New Grove* [211], vol. 20, pp. 1–3.

LYRIC FORMS, LYRIC METERS

489 Bec, Pierre. *La Lyrique française au moyen-âge (XIIe–XIIIe siècles): Contribution à une typologie des genres poétiques médiévaux.* 2 vols. Paris: Picard, 1977–78.

490 Bowra, C. M. *Greek Lyric Poetry from Alcman to Simonides.* 2nd ed., rev. Oxford: Clarendon Press, 1961.

491 Brittain, Frederick. "Introduction." *The Medieval Latin and Romance Lyric to A.D. 1300.* Cambridge: Cambridge University Press, 1937. Pp. 1–61.

492 Brook, G. L., ed. *The Harley Lyrics.* 3rd ed. Manchester: Manchester University Press, 1964.

❖ Cohen, Helen L. [324].

493 Dale, A. M. *The Lyric Meters of Greek Drama.* 2nd ed. Cambridge: Cambridge University Press, 1968. 228 pp.

494 Diehl, Patrick S. *The Medieval European Religious Lyric: An Ars Poetica.* Berkeley and Los Angeles: University of California Press, 1985. 357 pp.

495 Dronke, Peter. *Medieval Latin and the Rise of European Love Lyric.* 2nd ed. 2 vols. Oxford: Clarendon Press, 1968.

496 Durling, Robert M., ed. *Petrarch's Lyric Poems.* Cambridge, Mass.: Harvard University Press, 1976. 657 pp.

497 Erskine, John. *The Elizabethan Lyric*. New York: Macmillan, 1903.

498 Gennrich, Friedrich. *Grundriss einer Formenlehre des mittelalterlichen Liedes als Grundlage einer musikalischen Formenlehre des Liedes*. Halle: Niemeyer, 1932. 288 pp.

499 Headlam, Walter. "Greek Lyric Metres." *Journal of Hellenic Studies* 22 (1902): 209–27.

500 Hilka, Alfons, and Otto Schumann, eds. *Carmina Burana*. 3 vols. Heidelberg: Carl Winter, 1930–41.

501 Hinderer, Walter, ed. *Geschichte der deutschen Lyrik vom Mittelalter bis zur Gegenwart*. Stuttgart: Reclam, 1983. 659 pp.

❖   Honour, Margaret C. [774].

502 Ing, Catherine. *Elizabethan Lyrics: A Study of the Development of English Metrics and Their Relation to Poetic Effect*. London: Chatto & Windus, 1951; rpt. 1969. 252 pp.

503 Jeanroy, Alfred. *Les Origines de la poésie lyrique en France au Moyen Age*. 4th ed. Paris: H. Champion, 1965. 540 pp.

504 ———. *La Poésie lyrique des troubadours*. 2 vols. Paris: H. Didier, 1934.

505 Johnson, W. R. *The Idea of Lyric: Lyric Modes in Ancient and Modern Poetry*. Berkeley and Los Angeles: University of California Press, 1982. 214 pp.

❖   Le Gentil, Pierre [1285].

506 Lindley, David. *Lyric*. Critical Idiom Series, vol. 44. London: Methuen, 1985. 98 pp.

❖   Liu, James J. Y. [1475].

507 Maynard, Winifred. *Elizabethan Lyric Poetry and Its Music*. Oxford: Clarendon Press, 1986. 256 pp.

508 Oliver, Raymond. *Poems without Names: The English Lyric, 1200–1500*. Berkeley and Los Angeles: University of California Press, 1970. 165 pp.

509 Perloff, Marjorie. "Postmodernism and the Impasse of Lyric." In Perloff [550], pp. 172–200.

❖   Pollock, Sheldon I. [1453].

510 Ranawake, Silvia. *Höfische Strophenkunst: Vergleichende Untersuchungen zur Formentypologie von Minnesang und Trouvèrelied an der Wende zum Spätmittelalter*. Munich: Beck, 1970. 414 pp.

511 Rogers, William Elford. *The Three Genres and the Interpretation of Lyric*. Princeton: Princeton University Press, 1983. 277 pp.

512 Sayce, Olive. *The Medieval German Lyric, 1150–1300: The Development of Its Themes and Forms in Their European Context*. Oxford: Clarendon Press, 1982. 511 pp.

513 Spanke, Hans. *Bezeihungen zwischen romanischer und mittellateinischer Lyrik, mit besonderer Berücksichtigung der Metrik und Musik.* Berlin: Weidmannsche Buchhandlung, 1936.

514 ———. *Studien zur lateinischen und romanischen Lyrik des Mittelalters.* Ed. Ulrich Mölk. Hildesheim: Georg Olms, 1983. 472 pp.

Fourteen essays and a review of Gennrich are reprinted here; editor's foreword and index.

515 Watson, Burton. *Chinese Lyricism: Shih Poetry from the Second to the Twelfth Century.* New York: Columbia University Press, 1971.

516 Welsh, Andrew. *Roots of Lyric: Primitive Poetry and Modern Poetics.* Princeton: Princeton University Press, 1978. 276 pp.

FREE VERSE/*VERS LIBRE*

517 Beloof, Robert. "E. E. Cummings: The Prosodic Shape of His Poems." *DAI* 14, 7A (1954): 2342 (Northwestern).

518 Berry, Eleanor. "Syntactical and Metrical Structures in the Poetry of William Carlos Williams." *DAI* 42, 10A (1982): 4449 (Toronto).

519 Bollobás, Enikö. *Tradition and Innovation in American Free Verse: Whitman to Duncan.* Budapest: Akadémiai Kiadó, 1986. 328 pp.

❖ Brogan, T. V. F. [2], pp. 402ff.

520 Brooke-Rose, Christine. *A Structural Analysis of Pound's "Usura Canto": Jakobson's Method Extended and Applied to Free Verse.* The Hague: Mouton, 1976. 76 pp.

521 Closs, August. *Die freien Rhythmen in der deutschen Lyrik.* Bern: A. Francke, 1947. 198 pp.

522 Cureton, Richard D. "Visual Form in e. e. cummings' *No Thanks.*" *Word and Image* 2 (1986): 245–75.

523 Cushman, Stephen. *William Carlos Williams and the Meanings of Measure.* New Haven: Yale University Press, 1985. 161 pp.

524 Czerny, Z. "Le Vers libre français et son art structurel." In *Poetics I* [52], pp. 249–79.

525 Dondo, Mathurin M. *"Vers libre": A Logical Development of French Verse.* Paris: Champion, 1922. 87 pp.

526 Eliot, T. S. "Reflections on Vers Libre" [1917]; rpt. in his *To Criticize the Critic.* London: Faber & Faber, 1965. Pp. 183–89.

527 Ern, Lothar. *Freivers und Metrik: Zur Problematik der englischen Verswissenschaft.* Darmstadt: Blaeschke, 1970.

528 Frey, Hans-Jost, and Otto Lorenz. *Kritik des freien Verses*. Heidelberg: Schneider, 1980. 130 pp.

529 Grojnowski, Daniel. "Poétique du vers libre: Derniers vers de Jules Laforgue (1886)." *Revue d'Histoire Littéraire de la France* 84 (1984): 390–413.

❖   Gross, Harvey [764].

530 Hakak, Lev. "Modes of Organization in Modern Hebrew Free Verse." *DAI* 35, 10A (1975): 6714 (UCLA).

531 Hall, Donald, ed. *Claims for Poetry*. Ann Arbor: University of Michigan Press, 1982. 498 pp.

532 Hartman, Charles O. "At the Border." *Ohio Review*, no. 28 (1982): 81–92.

533 ———. *Free Verse: An Essay on Prosody*. Princeton: Princeton University Press, 1980. 199 pp.

534 Hass, Robert. "Creeley: His Metric." Rpt. in his *Twentieth-Century Pleasures: Prose on Poetry*. New York: Ecco, 1984. Pp. 150–60.

535 ———. "One Body: Some Notes on Form." *Antaeus* 30–31 (1978): 329–42; rpt. in his *Twentieth-Century Pleasures* [534], pp. 56–71.

536 Hellenbrecht, H. *Das Problem der freien Rhythmen*. Bern: Paul Haupt, 1931.

537 Helms, Alan. "Intricate Song's Lost Measure." *Sewanee Review* 87 (1979): 249–66.

538 Hollander, John. "Observations on the Experimental." In Hollander [22], pp. 227–44.

539 Hough, Graham. "Free Verse." *Proceedings of the British Academy* 43 (1957): 157–77.

❖   Hrushovski, Benjamin [224].

540 Jones, P. Mansell. *The Background of Modern French Poetry: Essays and Interviews*. Cambridge: Cambridge University Press, 1951. Part 2.

541 Justice, Donald. "The Free-Verse Line in Stevens." *Antaeus*, no. 53 (1984): 51–76.

542 Kell, Richard. "Note on Versification." *British Journal of Aesthetics* 3 (1963): 341–45.

543 Kwan-Terry, John. "Free Verse: A Prosodic Description of Its Development from Browning to T. S. Eliot." Ph.D. diss., Cambridge University, 1970.

544 Lowes, John Livingston. *Convention and Revolt in Poetry*. Boston: Houghton Mifflin, 1919.

545 Lucini, G. P. *Il Verso libero*. Milan, 1908.

546 McNaughton, William. "Ezra Pound's Metres and Rhythms." *PMLA* 78 (1963): 136–46.

547 Miller, Christanne. "The Iambic Pentameter Norm of Whitman's Free Verse." *Language and Style* 15 (1982): 289–324.

548 Monroe, Harriet. "The Free Verse Movement in America." *English Journal* 3 (1924): 691–705; rpt. in her *Poets and Their Art*. New York: Macmillan, 1926.

549 Morier, Henri. *Le Rythme du vers libre symboliste*. 3 vols. Geneva: Les Presses academiques, 1943–44.

550 Perloff, Marjorie. *The dance of the intellect: Studies in the Poetry of the Pound Tradition*. Cambridge: Cambridge University Press, 1985. 243 pp.

Collects ten of her essays on the varieties of modern verse.

551 Ramsey, Paul. "Free Verse: Some Steps Toward Definition." *Studies in Philology* 65 (1968): 98–108.

552 Sayre, Henry M. *The Visual Text of William Carlos Williams*. Urbana: University of Illinois Press, 1983. 152 pp.

❖ Scott, Clive [1162], chap. 7.

553 Taylor, Carole A. *A Poetics of Seeing: The Implications of Visual Form in Modern Poetry*. New York: Garland, 1985. 400 pp.

554 Wesling, Donald. "The Prosodies of Free Verse." *The New Poetries: Poetic Form since Coleridge and Wordsworth*. Lewisburg, Pa.: Bucknell University Press, 1985. Pp. 145–71.

VISUAL PROSODY

PATTERN POETRY

555 Adler, Jeremy. "*Technopaigneia, carmina figurata,* and *Bilder-Reime:* Seventeenth-century figured poetry in historical perspective." *Comparative Criticism: An Annual Journal* 4 (1982): 107–47.

556 Church, Margaret. "The First English Pattern Poems." *PMLA* 61 (1946): 636–50.

557 Doria, Charles. "Visual Writing Forms in Antiquity: The *Versus Intexti*." In Kostelanetz, ed. [577], pp. 63–92.

558 Elsky, Martin. "George Herbert's Pattern Poetry and the Materiality of Language: A New Approach to Renaissance Heiroglyphics." *ELH* 50 (1983): 245–60.

559 Ernst, Ulrich. "Die Entwicklung der optischen Poesie in Antike, Mittelalter und Neuzeit: Ein literatur-historisches Forschungsdesiderat." *Germanisch-Romanische Monatsschrift*, n.s. 26 (1976): 379–85.

560 ———. "Europäische Figurengedichte in Pyramidenform aus dem 16. und 17. Jahrhundert." *Euphorion* 72 (1982): 295–360.

561 Higgins, Dick. *Pattern Poetry: Guide to an Unknown Literature.* Albany: State University of New York Press, 1987. 275 pp.

562 Hollander, John. "The Poem in the Eye." In Hollander [22], pp. 245–87.

563 Korn, A. L. "Puttenham and the Oriental Pattern-Poem." *Comparative Literature* 6 (1954): 289–303.

564 Levitan, W. "Dancing at the End of the Rope: Optatian Porfyry and the Field of Roman Verse." *Transactions of the American Philological Association* 115 (1985): 245–69.

565 Newell, Kenneth B. *Pattern Poetry: A Historical Critique.* Boston: Marlborough House, 1976. 152 pp.

566 Peignot, Jérome. *Du Calligramme.* Paris: Chêne, 1978. 128 pp.

567 Schaller, Dieter. "Die karolingischen Figurengedichte des Cod. Bern 212." *Medium Aevum Vivum: Festschrift für W. Bulst.* Ed. H. R. Jauss and Dieter Schaller. Heidelberg: Carl Winter, 1960. Pp. 23–47.

568 Simonini, Laura, and Flaminio Gualdoni, eds. *Carmi figurati greci e latini.* Polenza-Macerata: La nuova Foglio, 1978.

569 Westerweel, Bart. *Patterns and Patterning: A Study of Four Poems by George Herbert.* Amsterdam: Rodopi, 1984. 274 pp.

CONCRETE POETRY

570 Bann, Stephen, ed. *Concrete Poetry: An International Anthology.* London: London Magazine, 1967.

571 Bayard, Caroline A. "Concrete Poetry in Canada and Quebec." *DAI* 39, 7A (1979): 4236.

572 Bohn, Willard. *The Aesthetics of Visual Poetry, 1914–1928.* Cambridge: Cambridge University Press, 1986. 228 pp.

❖ Brogan, T. V. F. [2], chap. 9.

573 Draper, R. P. "Concrete Poetry." *New Literary History* 2 (1971): 329–40.

574 Gumpel, Liselotte, ed. *"Concrete" Poetry from East and West Germany: The Language of Exemplarism and Experimentalism.* New Haven: Yale University Press, 1976.

575 Janecek, Gerald. *The Look of Russian Literature: Avant-Garde Visual Experiments, 1900–1930.* Princeton: Princeton University Press, 1984.

576 Kopfermann, Thomas, ed. *Theoretische Positionen zur konkreten Poesie.* Tübingen: Max Niemeyer, 1974.

577 Kostelanetz, Richard, ed. *Visual Literature Criticism: A New Collection*. Carbondale: Southern Illinois University Press, 1979. 192 pp.

578 McIIughes, Janet L. "The Poesis of Space: Prosodic Structures in Concrete Poetry." *Quarterly Journal of Speech* 63 (1977): 168–79.

579 Marcus, Aaron. "Introduction to the Visual Syntax of Concrete Poetry." *Visible Language* 8 (1974): 333–60.

580 *Poetics of the Avant Garde/Concrete Poetry*. Special issue of *Poetics Today* 3, no. 3 (1982).

581 Seaman, David W. *Concrete Poetry in France*. Ann Arbor: UMI Research Press, 1981. 356 pp.

582 Solt, Mary Ellen, and Willis Barnstone, eds. *Concrete Poetry: A World View*. Bloomington: Indiana University Press, 1969.

583 Steiner, Wendy. "*Res Poetica:* The Problematics of the Concrete Program." *The Colors of Rhetoric*. Chicago: University of Chicago Press, 1982. Pp. 197–219.

584 Tolman, Jon M. "The Context of a Vanguard: Toward a Definition of Concrete Poetry." In *Poetics of the Avant Garde* [580], pp 149–66

THE PROSE POEM

585 Alexander, Robert E. "The American Prose Poem, 1890–1980." *DAI* 44, 2A (1983): 489 (Wisconsin at Milwaukee).

586 Benedikt, Michael, ed. *The Prose Poem: An International Anthology*. New York: Dell, 1976.

587 Bernard, Suzanne. *Le Poème en prose de Baudelaire jusqu'à nos jours*. Paris: Librairie Nizet, 1959.

588 Caws, Mary Ann, and Hermine Riffaterre, eds. *The Prose Poem in France: Theory and Practice*. New York: Columbia University Press, 1983. 237 pp.

     Thirteen essays.

589 Fredman, Stephen. *Poet's Prose: The Crisis in American Verse*. Cambridge: Cambridge University Press, 1983. 173 pp.

590 Fülleborn, Ulrich. *Das deutsche Prosagedicht: Zu Theorie und Geschichte einer Gattung*. Munich: Wilhelm Fink, 1970. 59 pp.

591 ———, ed. *Deutsche Prosagedichte vom 18. Jahrhundert bis zur letzten Jahrhundertwende*. Munich: Wilhelm Fink, 1985. 295 pp.

592 ———. *Deutsche Prosagedichte des 20. Jahrhunderts*. Munich: Wilhelm Fink, 1976. 336 pp.

593   Keene, Dennis. *The Modern Japanese Prose Poem*. Princeton: Princeton University Press, 1980.

594   Lehman, David C. "The Marriage of Poetry and Prose." *DAI* 39, 8A (1979): 4938 (Columbia). 361 pp.

595   Scott, David. "La Structure spatiale de poème en prose: D'Aloysius Bertrand à Rimbaud." *Poétique*, no. 59 (1984): 295–300.

596   Silliman, Ron. "The New Sentence." *Talks: Hills 6/7*. San Francisco: Bob Perelman, 1980; abridged in *Claims for Poetry* [531], pp. 377–98; expanded into *The New Sentence*. New York: ROOF, 1987. 209 pp.

597   Slott, Kathryn E. "Poetics of the Nineteenth-Century French Prose Poem." *DAI* 41, 3A (1980): 1075 (Pennsylvania).

❖   Wesling, Donald. "Narrative of Grammar in the Prose Poem." In Wesling [554], pp. 172–200.

TWO

VERSE SYSTEMS

INDO-EUROPEAN

598 Campanile, Enrico. "Indogermanische Metrik und altirische Metrik." *Zeitschrift für Celtische Philologie* 37 (1979): 174–202.

599 Kurylowicz, Jerzy. "Indo-European Metrical Studies." In *Poetics I* [52], pp. 87–98.

600 ———. "The Quantitative Metre of Indo-European." *Indo-European and Indo-Europeans.* Ed. George Cardona et al. Philadelphia: University of Pennsylvania Press, 1970. Pp. 421–29.

601 McNeill, I. "The Metre of the Hittite Epic." *Anatolian Studies* 13 (1963): 237–42.

602 Meillet, Antoine. *Les Origines indo-européennes des mètres grecs.* Paris: Presses Universitaires de France, 1923. 79 pp.

603 Miller, D. Gary. "Traces of Indo-European Metre in Lydian." *Studies Presented to Professor Roman Jakobson by His Students.* Ed. Charles E. Gribble. Cambridge, Mass.: Slavica, 1968. Pp. 207–21.

604 Nagy, Gregory. *Comparative Studies in Greek and Indic Meter.* Cambridge, Mass.: Harvard University Press, 1974. 335 pp.

❖ Peabody, Berkley [316].

605 Schmitt, Rüdiger. *Dichtung und dichtersprache in indogermanischer Zeit.* Wiesbaden: Otto Harrassowitz, 1967. Chap. 10.

606 Vigorita, John F. "Indo-European Comparative Metrics." *DAI* 34, 11A (1974): 7216 (UCLA).

607 ———. "The Indo-European Origins of the Greek Hexameter and Distich." *Zeitschrift für Vergleichende Sprachforschung* 91 (1977): 288–99.

608 ———. "The Indo-European 12-Syllable Line." *Zeitschrift für Vergleichende Sprachforschung* 90 (1976): 37–46.

609 Watkins, Calvert. "Indo-European Metre and Archaic Irish Verse." *Celtica* 6 (1963): 194–249.

610 ———. "Indo-European Origins of a Celtic Metre." In *Poetics I* [52], pp. 99–118.

611 West, M. L. "Indo-European Metre." *Glotta* 51 (1973): 161–87.

612 ———. "Lydian Metre." *Kadmos* 11 (1972): 165–75.

613 Westphal, Rudolf. *Allgemeine Metrik der indogermanischen und semitischen Völker.* Berlin, 1892.

GREEK AND LATIN

BIBLIOGRAPHIES

614 *L'Année Philologique: Bibliographie critique et analytique de l'antiquité gréco-latine.*
     Paris: Les Belles Lettres, 1927– (annual).

     The annual bibliography for Classical studies; coverage begins 1924. See s.v.
     "Métrique, rythmique, prosodie."

615 Boeckh, August. "Metrik." *Encyklopädie und Methodologie der philologischen
     Wissenschaft.* 2nd ed. Leipzig, 1886. Pp. 813–18, 844–46.

616 Dale, A. M. "Greek Metric, 1936–1957." *Lustrum* 2 (1957): 5–51.

617 Getty, R. J. "Classical Latin Metre and Prosody, 1935–1960." *Lustrum* 8
     (1964): 103–60.

618 Harsh, Philip W. "Early Latin Meter and Prosody, 1935–1955." *Lustrum* 3
     (1958): 215–50.

619 Gleditsch, Hugo. "Jahresbericht über die Erscheinungen auf dem Gebiete
     der griechischen und römischen Metrik," *Jahresbericht über die Fortschritte der
     klassischen Altertumswissenschaft* 102 (1900): 1–64, 125 (1905): 1–85, 144 (1909):
     75–156.

     Three extended bibliographic-review essays covering work 1892–1907 and
     extending the earlier surveys by R. Klotz in 36 (1883): 289–453, 48 (1886):
     55–160, and 69 (1891): 199–250.

620 Kalinka, Ernst. "Griechisch-römische Metrik und Rhythmik im letzten
     Vierteljahrhundert." *Jahresbericht über die Fortschritte der klassischen Altertum-
     swissenschaft* 250 (1935): 290–507; supplemented in 256 (1937): 1–126, 257
     (1937): 1–160.

621 McGuire, Martin R. P. *Introduction to Medieval Latin Studies: A Syllabus and
     Bibliographical Guide.* Washington D.C.: Catholic University of America
     Press, 1964. 152 pp.

622 Packard, D. W., and T. Meyers. *A Bibliography of Homeric Scholarship.* Mal-
     ibu, Calif.: Undena Publications, 1974.

623 Parker, L. P. E. "Greek Metric, 1957–1970." *Lustrum* 15 (1970): 37–98.

624 West, M. L. "Greek Poetry, 2000–700 B.C." *Classical Quarterly* 23 (1973):
     179–92.

ENCYCLOPEDIAS, DICTIONARIES

625 *Der kleine Pauly: Lexikon der Antike.* 5 vols. Stuttgart: A. Druckenmüller,
     1964–75.

626 *Paulys Realencyclopädie der classischen Altertumswissenschaft.* Ed. A. Pauly, G. Wissowa, W. Kroll, and K. Mittelhaus. 24 vols. (A-Q), 10 vols. (R-Z, Series 2), and 15 vols. (Supplements). Stuttgart: J. B. Metzler, 1894–1978.

HISTORIES

627 *Cambridge History of Classical Literature.* 2 vols. Vol. 1, *Greek Literature*, ed. P. E. Easterling and B. M. W. Knox; vol. 2, *Latin Literature*, ed. E. J. Kenney. Cambridge: Cambridge University Press, 1982–85.

CLASSICAL GREEK

628 Allen, W. Sidney. *Accent and Rhythm. Prosodic Features of Latin and Greek: A Study in Accentuation.* Cambridge: Cambridge University Press, 1973. 394 pp.

629 ———. "On Quantity and Quantitative Verse." *In Honour of Daniel Jones.* Ed. David Abercrombie et al. London: Longmans, 1964. Pp. 3–15.

630 ———. *Vox Graeca: A Guide to the Pronunciation of Classical Greek.* 3rd ed. Cambridge: Cambridge University Press, 1987. 179 pp.

631 Bentley, Richard. *Schediasma de metris Terentianus.* Cambridge, 1726.

632 Boeckh, August. "De metris Pindari." In his *Pindari opera.* Leipzig, 1811.

633 ———. *De metris Pindari, libri III.* Leipzig, 1814. 562 pp.

634 Bowra, C. M. "Metre." *A Companion to Homer.* Ed. Alan J. B. Wace and F. H. Stubbings. London: Macmillan, 1962. Pp. 19–25.

635 Cole, A. Thomas. "Classical Greek and Latin [Versification]." In Wimsatt, ed. [60], pp. 66–88.

636 Dale, A. M. *Collected Papers.* Cambridge: Cambridge University Press, 1969. 307 pp.

❖ ———. *The Lyric Meters of Greek Drama* [493].

637 Denniston, J. D. "Metre, Greek." *Oxford Classical Dictionary.* Ed. N. G. L. Hammond and H. H. Scullard. 2nd ed. Oxford: Clarendon Press, 1970. Pp. 679–84.

638 Devine, A. M., and L. D. Stephens. *Language and Metre: Resolution, Porson's Bridge, and Their Prosodic Basis.* Chico, Calif.: Scholars Press, 1984. 147 pp.

639 ———. "Preliminaries to an Explicit Theory of Greek Meter." *Transactions of the American Philological Association* 107 (1977): 103–29.

640 ———. "Stress in Greek?" *Transactions of the American Philological Association* 115 (1985): 125–52.

641 ———. "Towards a New Theory of Greek Prosody: The Suprasyllabic Rules." *Transactions of the American Philological Association* 112 (1982): 33–63.

642 Drexler, Hans. *Hexameterstudien*. Salamanca: n.p., 1953. 129 pp.

643 Gleditsch, Hugo. *Metrik der Griechen und Römer mit einem Anhang über die Musik der Griechen*. 3rd ed. Handbüch der klassischen Altertumswissenschaft, vol. 2, part 3. Leipzig, 1901.

644 Grotjahn, Rüdiger, ed. *Hexameter Studies*. Bochum: Brockmeyer, 1981. 262 pp.

   With a long annotated bibliography on statistical studies of the Classical hexameter, pp. 226–62.

❖ Guggenheimer, Eva H. [114].

645 Halporn, James W., Martin Ostwald, and Thomas G. Rosenmeyer. *The Meters of Greek and Latin Poetry.*. 2nd ed., rev. Norman: University of Oklahoma Press, 1980. 137 pp.

646 Hardie, W. R. *Res Metrica: An Introduction to the Study of Greek and Roman Versification*. Oxford: Clarendon Press, 1920.

647 Hephaestion. *Enchiridion peri metron*. Ed. Maximilian Consbruch. Leipzig, 1906, rpt. Stuttgart: B. G. Teubner, 1971. 420 pp. Eng. trans. J. M. van Ophuijsen. *Hephaestion on Metre: A Translation and Commentary*. Mnemosyne, supp. vol. 100. Leiden: E. J. Brill, 1987.

648 Hermann, Gottfried. *Elementa doctrinae metricae*. Leipzig, 1816.

649 ———. *De metris graecorum et romanorum*. Leipzig, 1796.

650 Hoffmann, Johann B., and Hans Rubenbauer. *Wörterbuch der grammatischen und metrischen Terminologie*. 2nd ed. Heidelberg: Carl Winter, 1963. 78 pp.

651 Koster, W. J. W. *Traité de métrique grecque, suivi d'un précis de métrique latine*. 4th ed. Leyden: A. W. Sijthoff, 1966. 388 pp.

652 ———, ed. *Tractatus graeci de re metrica inediti*. Paris, 1922.

653 Maas, Paul. *Greek Metre*. Trans. Hugh Lloyd-Jones. 2nd ed. Oxford: Clarendon Press, 1966. 116 pp.

654 O'Neill, E. G., Jr. "The Localization of Metrical Word-types in the Greek Hexameter." *Yale Classical Studies* 8 (1942): 103–78.

❖ Parry, Milman [315].

❖ Pighi, G. B. [51].

655 Porter, H. N. "The Early Greek Hexameter." *Yale Classical Studies* 12 (1951): 1–63.

656 Scott, William C. *Musical Design in Aeschylean Theater*. Hanover, N.H.: University Press of New England, 1984. 216 pp.

657 Snell, Bruno. *Griechische Metrik*. 4th ed. Göttingen: Vandenhoeck & Ruprecht, 1982.

❖ Stanford, W. B. [82].

658 Thalmann, William G. *Conventions of Form and Thought in Early Greek Epic Poetry*. Baltimore: Johns Hopkins University Press, 1984. 262 pp.

659 Traverse, S. E. "Ictus Metricus: Phonological, Historical, and Comparative Studies in Greek and Latin Meter." *DAI* 41, 11A (1981): 4697 (Toronto).

660 Wahlström, Erik. *Accentual Responsion in Greek Strophic Poetry*. Helsinki: Societas Scientiarum Fennica, 1970.

661 West, M. L. *Greek Metre*. Oxford: Clarendon Press, 1982. 208 pp.

662 ———. *Introduction to Greek Metre*. Oxford: Clarendon Press, 1987. 92 pp.

663 ———. *Studies in Greek Elegy and Iambus*. Berlin and New York: De Gruyter, 1974. 198 pp.

664 ———. "Three Topics in Greek Metre." *Classical Quarterly* 32 (1982): 281–97.

665 White, John William. *The Verse of Greek Comedy*. London: Macmillan, 1912. 479 pp.

666 Wilamowitz-Möllendorff, Ulrich von. *Griechische Verskunst*. 2nd ed. Berlin, 1921; rpt. Darmstadt: Gentner, 1968. 630 pp.

667 Wyatt, William F. *Metrical Lengthening in Homer*. Rome: Edizioni dell'Ateneo, 1969. 248 pp.

Classical Latin

668 Beare, William. "The Meaning of *Ictus* as Applied to Latin Verse." *Hermathena*, no. 81 (1953): 29–40.

669 Bennett, Charles E. "What Was Ictus in Latin Prosody?" *American Journal of Philology* 19 (1898): 361–83. Reply by G. L. Hendrickson in 20 (1899): 198–210; rejoinders, 412–34.

670 Cole, A. Thomas. "The Saturnian Verse." *Yale Classical Studies* 21 (1969): 3–73.

671 Cooper, C. G. *An Introduction to the Latin Hexameter*. Melbourne: Macmillan, 1952. 70 pp.

672 Crusius, Friedrich. *Römische Metrik: Ein Einfürhung*. 8th ed. Rev. Hans Rubenbauer. Munich: Max Hueber, 1967.

673 Devine, A. M., and L. D. Stephens. *Two Studies in Latin Phonology*. Saratoga, Calif.: Anma Libri, 1977. 237 pp.

674 Drexler, Hans. *Einführung in die romische Metrik*. Darmstadt: Wissenschaftliche Buchgellschaft, 1967.

675 Duckworth, G. E. "Variety and Repetition in Vergil's Hexameters." *Transactions of the American Philological Association* 95 (1964): 9–65.

676 ———. *Vergil and Classical Hexameter Poetry: A Study in Metrical Variety*. Ann Arbor: University of Michigan Press, 1969.

677 Halporn, James W., and Martin Ostwald. *Lateinische Metrik*. 3rd ed. Göttingen: Vandenhoeck & Ruprecht, 1982. 62 pp.

678 Herescu, N. I. *La Poésie latine: Étude des structures phoniques*. Paris: Les Belles Lettres, 1960. 227 pp.

679 Knight, W. F. Jackson. *Accentual Symmetry in Vergil*. 2nd ed. Oxford: Clarendon Press, 1950.

680 Liénard, Edmond. *Répertoires prosodiques et métriques*. Brussels: Éditions de l'Université de Bruxelles, 1978. 204 pp.

681 Lindsay, W. M. *Early Latin Verse*. Oxford: Clarendon Press, 1922; rpt. London: Oxford University Press, 1968. 372 pp.

682 Mountford, J. F. "Metre, Latin." *Oxford Classical Dictionary* [637], pp. 684–85.

683 Norden, Eduard. "Die malarischen Mittel des Vergilischen Hexameters." *Aeneis Buch VI*. Ed. E. Norden. 4th ed. Stuttgart: B. G. Teubner, 1957. Pp. 413–34 et seq.

❖ ———. [126].

❖ Peabody, Berkley [316].

684 Platnauer, Maurice. *Latin Elegiac Verse: A Study of the Metrical Usages of Tibullus, Propertius & Ovid*. Cambridge: Cambridge University Press, 1951; rpt. Hamden, Conn.: Archon, 1971. 121 pp.

685 Poe, Joe P. *Caesurae in the Hexameter Line of Latin Elegiac Verse*. Wiesbaden: F. Steiner, 1974. 91 pp.

686 Polheim, Karl. *Die lateinische Reimprosa*. Berlin: Weidmannsche Buchhandlung, 1925. 539 pp.

687 Postgate, J. P. *Prosodia Latina: An Introduction to Classical Verse*. Oxford, 1923.

688 Schumann, Otto. *Lateinsiches Hexameter-Lexikon: Dichterisches Formelgut von Ennius bis zum Archipoeta*. 6 vols. Munich: Monumenta Germaniae Historica, 1979–83.

689 Sparrow, John. *Half-Lines and Repetitions in Virgil*. Oxford: Clarendon Press, 1931.

690 Starobinski, Jean. *Les Mots sous les mots*. Trans. Olivia Emmet as *Words upon Words*. New Haven: Yale University Press, 1979. 129 pp.

691 Wilkinson, L. P. *Golden Latin Artistry*. Cambridge: Cambridge University Press, 1963; rpt. Norman: University of Oklahoma Press, 1985. 283 pp.

MEDIEVAL LATIN

692 Baldwin, C. S. *Medieval Rhetoric and Poetic (to 1400) Interpreted from Representative Works*. New York: Macmillan, 1928; rpt. St. Clair Shores, Mich.: Scholarly Press, 1972. 321 pp.

❖ Beare, William [8].

693 Bolton, W. F. *A History of Anglo-Latin Literature, 597–1066*. 2 vols. Princeton: Princeton University Press, 1967.

❖ Brittain, Frederick [491].

694 Crocker, Richard L. *The Early Medieval Sequence*. Berkeley and Los Angeles: University of California Press, 1977. 470 pp.

695 Curtius, E. R. *European Literature and the Latin Middle Ages*. Trans. Willard Trask. Princeton: Princeton University Press, 1953.

❖ Dronke, Peter [495].

696 Jones, Charles W. "Carolingian Aesthetics: Why Modular Verse?" *Viator* 6 (1975): 309–40.

697 Jones, Charles W., C. B. Kendall, and M. H. King, eds. *Bedae Venerabilis Opera: Opera Didascalia*. Corpus Christianorum, Series Latina, vol. 123A. Turnhout: Brepols, 1975.

698 Kabell, Aage, ed. *Iacobus Nicholai de Dacia. Liber de distinccione metrorum*. Uppsala: Almqvist & Wiksell, 1967. 207 pp.

699 Keil, Heinrich, ed. *Scriptores arte metrica*. Vol. 6 of his *Grammatici Latini*. 7 vols. and supp. Leipzig, 1857–80; rpt. Hildesheim: Georg Olms, 1961.

Standard texts of most of the Medieval Latin prosody manuals.

700 Klopsch, Paul. *Einführung in die mittellateinische Verslehre*. Darmstadt: Wissenschaftliche Buchgesellschaft, 1972. 117 pp.

701 Knight, W. F. Jackson. *St. Augustine's "De Musica": A Synopsis*. London: Orthological Institute, 1949; rpt. Westport, Conn.: Hyperion, 1979. 125 pp.

702 Lapidge, Michael. "Aldhelm's Poetry and Old English Verse." *Comparative Literature* 31 (1979): 209–31.

703 Lapidge, Michael, James L. Rosier, and Neil Wright, eds. *Aldhelm: The Poetic Works*. Woodbridge, Eng.: D. S. Brewer, 1985. 274 pp.

Especially Wright's appendix, "Aldhelm's Prose Writings on Metrics," pp. 181–219.

704 Law, Vivien. "The Study of Latin Grammar in Eighth-Century Southumbria." *Anglo-Saxon England, 12.* Ed. Peter Clemoes. Cambridge: Cambridge University Press, 1983. Pp. 43–71.

705 Lawler, Traugott, ed. *The "Parisiana Poetria" of John of Garland.* New Haven: Yale University Press, 1974. 352 pp.

❖ Lewis, Charlton M. [726].

706 Löfstedt, Bengt, ed. *Bonifatii (Wynfreth): Ars grammatica: accedit Ars metrica.* Corpus Christianorum, Series Latina, vol. 133B. Turnhout: Brepols, 1980. 140 pp.

707 Mari, Giovanni. "Ritmo latino e terminologia ritmica medievale." *Studi di Filologia Romanza* 8 (1901): 35–88.

708 ———, ed. *I trattati medievali di ritmica latina.* Milan, 1899; rpt. Bologna: Forni, 1971. 124 pp.

Texts of eight Medieval Latin treatises on the *ars rithmica.*

709 Meyer, Wilhelm. *Gessamelte Abhandlungen zur mittellateinischen Rhythmik.* 3 vols. Leipzig, 1905–36; rpt. (with foreword by Walter Bulst) Hildesheim: Georg Olms, 1970.

His collected works on Medieval Latin versification.

710 Morgan, Margery M. "A Treatise in Cadence." *MLR* 47 (1952): 156–64.

711 Murphy, James J. *Rhetoric in the Middle Ages: A History of Rhetorical Theory from St. Augustine to the Renaissance.* Berkeley and Los Angeles: University of California Press, 1974, rpt. 1981. Chaps. 4–5.

712 Norberg, Dag. *Introduction à l'étude de la versification latine médiévale.* Stockholm: Almqvist & Wiksell, 1958. 218 pp.

713 ———. *La Poésie latine rythmique du haut Moyen Age.* Stockholm: Almqvist & Wiksell, 1954. 119 pp.

714 Palmer, Robert B. "Bede as Textbook Writer: A Study of His *De Arte Metrica.*" *Speculum* 34 (1959): 573–84.

715 Rudmose-Brown, T. B. "Some Medieval Latin Metres: Their Ancestry and Progeny." *Hermathena,* no. 53 (1939): 29–58.

716 Schaller, Dieter. "Bauformeln für akzent-rhythmische Vers und Strophen." *Mittellateinisches Jahrbuch* 14 (1979): 9–21.

717 Schlicher, John J. "The Origin of Rhythmical Verse in Late Latin." Ph.D. diss., University of Chicago, 1900.

718 Strecker, Karl. "Poetry." *Introduction to Medieval Latin.* 2nd ed. trans. and rev. Robert B. Palmer. Berlin: Wiedmann, 1963. Pp. 71–85.

719 Wright, Neil. "The Anglo-Latin Hexameter: Theory and Practice c. 600–c. 800." Ph.D. diss., Cambridge University, 1981.

TRANSITION FROM LATIN TO THE EUROPEAN VERNACULARS

❖ Beare, William [8].

720 Burger, Michel. *Recherches sur la structure et l'origine des vers romans.* Geneva: E. Droz, 1957. 188 pp.

721 Frank, István. *Trouvères et Minnesänger.* Saarbrücken: West-Ost Verlag, 1952.

722 Gillespie, G. "Origins of Romance Lyrics: A Review." *Yearbook of Comparative and General Literature* 16 (1967): 16–32.

723 Harper, Anthony J. "Renaissance Verse Reform and the German Poetry of the Seventeenth Century." *Neuphilologische Mitteilungen* 79 (1978): 426–37.

❖ Jeanroy, Alfred [503].

724 Kawczynski, Maximilian. *Essai comparatif sur l'origine et l'histoire des rythmes.* Paris, 1889. 220 pp.

725 Kurylowicz, Jerzy. "Latin and Germanic Metre." *English and German Studies* 2 (1948–49): 34–38; rpt. in his *Esquisses linguistiques.* Wroclaw: Zaklad Narodowy im. Ossliński ch, 1960. Pp. 294–98.

726 Lewis, Charlton M. *The Foreign Sources of Modern English Versification.* New Haven: Yale University Press, 1898.

727 Mölk, Ulrich. "Vers latin et vers roman." In *GRLM* [1103], vol. 1, *Généralities,* pp. 467–82.

728 Pulgram, Ernst. *Latin-Romance Phonology: Prosodics and Metrics.* Munich: Wilhelm Fink, 1975. 301 pp.

729 Purczinsky, J. "Germanic Influence in the *Saint Eulalia.*" *Romance Philology* 19 (1965): 271–75.

❖ Ranawake, Silvia [510].

730 Sheldon, Edward S. "Some Remarks on the Origin of Romance Versification." *Anniversary Papers by Colleagues and Pupils of George Lyman Kittredge.* Boston: Ginn, 1913. Pp. 37–46.

731 Spanke, Hans. *Deutsche und französische Dichtung des Mittelalters.* Stuttgart: W. Kohlhammer, 1943.

732 Thomas, Walter. *Le Décasyllabe roman et sa fortune en europe.* Lille, 1904. 201 pp.

IMITATIONS OF CLASSICAL METERS
IN MODERN LANGUAGES

733   Attridge, Derek. *Well-Weighed Syllables: Elizabethan Verse in Classical Metres.* Cambridge: Cambridge University Press, 1974; rpt. 1979. 258 pp.

734   Baxter, Arthur H. *The Introduction of Classical Metres into Italian Poetry and Their Development to the Beginning of the Nineteenth Century.* Baltimore, 1901. 33 pp.

735   Bennett, W[alter]. *German Verse in Classical Metres.* The Hague: Mouton, 1963. 315 pp.

736   Brückner, C. *Über die Nachahmung der griechischen und lateinischen Dichter in der deutsche Sprache.* Berlin, 1852.

❖   Burgi, Richard [1359].

737   Carducci, Giosue. *Odi barbare.* 2nd ed. Rome, 1878. With introduction by Giuseppe Chiabrini.

738   Censi Mancia, Carlo. *Saggio sulla poesia quantitativa antica e moderna.* Macerata: Stampato da A. Bricchi, 1955.

739   Dunn, Catherine M. "A Survey of the Experiments in Quantitative Verse in the English Renaissance." *DAI* 28, 1A (1967): 193 (UCLA).

❖   Elwert, W. Theodor. *Italienische Metrik* [1316], pp. 148–74.

740   Elze, Karl. *Der englische Hexameter.* Dessau, 1867.

741   Hellmuth, Hans-Heinrich, and Joachim Schroeder, eds. *Die Lehre von der Nachahmung der antike Versmasse im Deutschen in Quellenschriften des 18. und 19. Jahrhunderts.* Munich: Wilhelm Fink, 1976. 558 pp.

742   Herrera Zapién, Tarsicio. *La métrica latinizante: Estudio acerca de la teoría y la práctica de los metros latinos en italiano, frances, inglés, alemán y castellano.* Ciudad Universitaria, Mexico: Universidad Nacional Autonoma de Mexico, Instituto de Investigaciones Filologicas, 1975. 225 pp.

743   Kabell, Aage. *Metrische Studien III: Antike Form sich nähernd.* Uppsala: Lundequistska bokhandeln, 1960.

❖   Omond, T. S. [761], app. A.

744   Park, Ben A. "The Quantitative Experiments of the Renaissance and after as a Problem in Comparative Metrics." *DAI* 29, 3A (1968): 905 (Oklahoma).

745   Wölk, Konrad. *Geschichte und Kritik des englischen Hexameters.* Berlin, 1909. 146 pp.

IRISH AND WELSH

❖ Campanile, Enrico [598].

746 Davies, A. Talfan. "William Barnes, Gerard Manley Hopkins, Dylan Thomas: The Influence of Welsh Prosody on Modern English Poetry." *Proceedings of the Third Congress of the Comparative Literature Association.* The Hague: Mouton, 1962. Pp. 90–122.

747 Davies, J. Glyn. *Welsh Metrics.* London: Constable, 1911.

748 Dunn, Charles W. "Celtic [Versification]." In Wimsatt, ed. [60], pp. 136–47.

749 Knott, Eleanor. *An Introduction to Irish Syllabic Poetry of the Period 1200–1600.* 2nd. ed. Dublin: Dublin Institute for Advanced Studies, 1957.

750 Lehmann, Ruth. *Early Irish Verse.* Austin: University of Texas Press, 1982.

See the introduction and notes.

751 Matonis, A. T. E. "The Welsh Bardic Grammars and the Western Grammatical Tradition." *Modern Philology* 79 (1981): 121–45.

752 Meyer, Kuno. *A Primer of Irish Metrics.* Dublin, 1909. 63 pp.

❖ Meyer, Wilhelm [709]. "Die Verskunst der Iren in rhythmischen lateinischen Gedichten." Vol. 3, pp. 303–28.

753 Murphy, Gerard. *Early Irish Metrics.* Dublin: Royal Irish Academy, 1961.

754 O Cuív, Brian. "Metrics and Irish Phonology." *Occasional Papers in Linguistics and Language Learning* 6 (1979): 108–23.

755 Parry, Thomas. *A History of Welsh Literature.* Trans. H. Idris Bell. Oxford: Clarendon Press, 1955. 534 pp.

756 Rowlands, Eurys. "*Cynghanedd*, Metre, Prosody." *A Guide to Welsh Literature.* Ed. A. O. H. Jarman et al. Swansea: Davies, 1979. Vol. 2, pp. 202–17.

757 Thurneysen, Rudolf. "Mittelirische Verslehren." *Irische Texte.* Ed. Whitney Stokes and E. Windisch. 3 vols. Leipzig, 1891. Vol. 3, pp. 1–182.

758 Travis, James. *Early Celtic Versecraft: Origin, Development, Diffusion.* Ithaca: Cornell University Press, 1973. 166 pp.

❖ Watkins, Calvert [609].

ENGLISH

BIBLIOGRAPHIES

❖ Brogan, T. V. F. [2].

❖ *Eidos* [3].

759 Greenfield, Stanley B., and Fred C. Robinson. *A Bibliography of Publications on Old English Literature to the End of 1972*. Toronto: University of Toronto Press, 1980.

S.v. "Prosodic Studies," pp. 103–9, 195–96, etc.

760 Hammond, Eleanor P. "Linguistics and Versification." *Chaucer: A Bibliographical Manual*. New York: Macmillan, 1908; rpt. 1933. Pp. 464–509.

761 Omond, T. S. *English Metrists: Being a Sketch of English Prosodical Criticism from Elizabethan Times to the Present Day*. Oxford: Clarendon Press, 1921. 327 pp.

Confines itself to works (on English) written in English but offers long commentaries on earlier writers and includes a separate bibliography of English imitations of classical quantitative meters.

HISTORIES

762 Allen, Gay Wilson. *American Prosody*. New York: American Book Company, 1935; rpt. New York: Octagon, 1978. 328 pp.

Surveys the versification of eleven (eighteenth- and nineteenth-century) American poets, Freneau through Dickinson.

763 Chambers, E. K. *English Literature at the Close of the Middle Ages*. Oxford: Clarendon Press, 1945. 247 pp.

764 Gross, Harvey. *Sound and Form in Modern Poetry: A Study of Prosody from Thomas Hardy to Robert Lowell*. Ann Arbor: University of Michigan Press, 1964.

The most recent book-length treatment of prosody in twentieth-century poetry.

765 Pearsall, Derek. *Old English and Middle English Poetry*. London: Routledge & Kegan Paul, 1977. 352 pp.

766 Piper, William Bowman. *The Heroic Couplet*. Cleveland: Case Western Reserve University Press, 1969. 465 pp.

Still the most extensive treatment of eighteenth-century prosody.

767 Saintsbury, George. *A History of English Prosody From the Twelfth Century to the Present Day*. 3 vols. London: Macmillan, 1906–10; 2nd ed. 1923; rpt. New York: Russell & Russell, 1961.

Saintsbury is often excellent when discussing poetry after 1500 but eccentric and unreliable when discussing theory: perhaps better avoided except for discussion of a specific poet. Particularly avoid his discussions of Old and Middle English.

768 Schipper, Jakob. *Englische Metrik in historischer und systematischer Entwicklung dargestellt*. 3 vols. Bonn: Emil Strauss, 1881–88.

Weighted toward Old and Middle English (his specialty), but still the soundest and most extensive treatment of the subject.

769 ———. *A History of English Versification*. Oxford: Clarendon Press, 1910; rpt. New York: AMS, 1971. 390 pp.

The fullest one-volume study of English versification. Still indispensable despite intimidating organization.

770 Tarlinskaja, M. G. *English Verse: Theory and History*. The Hague: Mouton, 1976. 351 pp.

Proposes a typology of English meters based on statistical analysis of 100,000 lines of verse, thirteenth through nineteenth centuries: 230 pages of text interpret 103 pages of tables and charts.

771 Thompson, John. *The Founding of English Metre*. New York: Columbia University Press, 1961; rpt. 1988. 192 pp.

Currently the best account of the emergence of modern English meter in the Renaissance.

772 Woods, Suzanne. *Natural Emphasis: English Versification from Chaucer to Dryden*. San Marino, Calif.: Huntington Library Press, 1984. 310 pp.

STANZA INDEXES

773 Cutler, John L. "A Manual of Middle English Stanzaic Patterns." 2 vols. Ph.D. diss., Ohio State University, 1949. 546 pp.

774 Honour, Margaret C. "The Metrical Derivations of the Medieval English Lyric." 2 vols. Diss., Yale University, 1949. *DAI* 31, 5A (1970): 2346.

Vol. 2 cross-indexes the metrical patterns of lyrics in Latin, Provençal, French, and English.

❖ Schipper, Jakob. *History of English Versification* [769].

No complete stanza index to modern English poetry yet exists; in its absence, Schipper still gives the most extensive data.

GENERAL STUDIES

775   Alden, R. M. *English Verse: Specimens Illustrating Its Principles and History.* 2nd ed. New York: Holt, 1929; rpt. New York: AMS, 1970. 441 pp.

776   ———. "The Mental Side of Metrical Form." *Modern Language Review* 9 (1914): 298–308.

777   Baroway, Israel. "The Accentual Theory of Hebrew Prosody: A Further Study in the Renaissance Interpretation of Biblical Form." *ELH* 17 (1950): 115–35.

778   ———. "The Bible as Poetry in the English Renaissance: An Introduction." *JEGP* 32 (1933): 447–80.

779   Barry, M. Martin, Sister. *An Analysis of the Prosodic Structure of Selected Poems of T. S. Eliot.* Rev. ed. Washington, D.C.: Catholic University of America Press, 1969.

780   Bate, W. Jackson. *The Stylistic Development of Keats.* New York: MLA, 1945; rpt. New York: Humanities, 1962. 214 pp.

781   Berdan, John M. *Early Tudor Poetry, 1485–1547.* New York: Macmillan, 1920.

782   Bernard, J. E., Jr. *The Prosody of the Tudor Interlude.* New Haven: Yale University Press, 1939; rpt. Hamden, Conn.: Archon, 1969. 225 pp.

783   Bernhart, Walter. "Complexity and Metricality." *Poetics* 12 (1974): 113–42.

784   Beum, Robert. *The Poetic Art of William Butler Yeats.* New York: Ungar, 1969. 161 pp.

785   Blackmur, R. P. "Lord Tennyson's Scissors, 1912–1950." *Kenyon Review* 14 (1952): 1–20; rpt. in his *Form and Value in Modern Poetry.* New York: Doubleday, 1957. Pp. 369–88.

❖   Booth, Stephen [431].

786   Brown, Calvin S. "Monosyllables in English Verse." *Studies in English Literature 1500–1900* 3 (1963): 473–91.

787   Clinton-Baddeley, V. C. *Words for Music.* Cambridge: Cambridge University Press, 1941. 168 pp.

788   Coleridge, Samuel Taylor. *Biographia Literaria.* London, 1817. Ed. James Engell and W. Jackson Bate. 2 vols. Princeton: Princeton University Press, 1983. Chap. 18.

789   Creek, Herbert L. "Rising and Falling Rhythms in English Verse." *PMLA* 35 (1920): 76–90.

790   Crystal, David. "Intonation and Metrical Theory." *Transactions of the Philological Society,* 1971, pp. 1–33.

791   Eliot, T. S. *The Music of Poetry.* Glasgow, 1942; rpt. in his *On Poetry and Poets.* London: Faber & Faber, 1957, rpt. 1961. Pp. 17–33.

792 Fowler, Roger. *The Language of Literature: Some Linguistic Contributions to Criticism*. London: Routledge & Kegan Paul, 1971. 256 pp.

793 ———. "What Is Metrical Analysis?" *Anglia* 86 (1968): 280–320; rpt. in his *The Languages of Literature* [792].

794 Freer, Coburn. *The Poetics of Jacobean Drama*. Baltimore: Johns Hopkins University Press, 1981. 288 pp.

795 Fucks, William. "Possibilities of Exact Style Analysis." *Patterns of Literary Style*. Ed. Joseph Strelka. University Park: Penn State University Press, 1971. Pp. 51–76.

796 Gardner, Helen. *The Art of T. S. Eliot*. London: Cresset Press, 1949, rpt. 1979.

797 Halpern, Martin. "On the Two Chief Metrical Modes in English." *PMLA* 77 (1962): 177–86.

798 Hamm, Victor. "Meter and Meaning." *PMLA* 69 (1954): 695–710.

799 Hatcher, Harlan H. *The Versification of Robert Browning*. Columbus: Ohio State University Press, 1928. 195 pp.

800 Hickson, Elizabeth C. *The Versification of Thomas Hardy*. Philadelphia: n.p., 1931. 129 pp.

❖ Hollander, John. *Vision and Resonance* [22].

801 Housman, A. E. *The Name and Nature of Poetry*. Cambridge: Cambridge University Press, 1933. 51 pp.

802 Jorgens, Elise B. *The Well-Tun'd Word: Musical Interpretations of English Poetry, 1597–1631*. Minneapolis: University of Minnesota Press, 1982. 298 pp.

803 Justice, Donald. "Meters and Memory." *Antaeus*, nos. 30–31 (1978): 314–20.

804 Kellog, George A. "Bridges' *Milton's Prosody* and Renaissance Metrical Theory." *PMLA* 68 (1953): 268–85.

❖ Ker, W. P. [29].

805 Kuhn, Ursula. "Prosody." *English Literary Terms in Poetological Texts of the Sixteenth Century*. 3 vols. Salzburg: Salzburg Institut für englische Sprache und Literatur, 1974. Vol. 2, pp. 453–70.

806 Legouis, Émile. *A Short Parallel between French and English Versification*. Cambridge: Bowes & Bowes, 1925. 18 pp.

❖ Lewis, Charlton M. [726].

807 Lewis, C. S. "Metre." *Review of English Literature* 1 (1960): 45–50; rpt. in his *Selected Literary Essays*. Ed. Walter Hooper. Cambridge: Cambridge University Press, 1969. Pp. 280–85.

808 Lowbury, Edward, Timothy Salter, and Alison Young. *Thomas Campion: Poet, Composer, Physician*. New York: Barnes & Noble, 1970.

809 Mace, D. T. "Musical Humanism, the Doctrine of Rhythmus, and the Saint Cecelia Odes of Dryden." *Journal of the Warburg and Courtauld Institute* 27 (1964): 251–92.

810 Malof, Joseph. "Meter as Organic Form." *Modern Language Quarterly* 27 (1966): 3–17.

811 ———. "The Native Rhythm of English Meters." *Texas Studies in Literature and Language* 5 (1964): 580–94.

812 Melton, W. F. *The Rhetoric of John Donne's Verse*. Baltimore, 1906. 206 pp.

❖ Nowottny, Winifred [49].

813 Oras, Ants. *Pause Patterns in Elizabethan and Jacobean Drama: An Experiment in Prosody*. Gainesville: University of Florida Press, 1960. 90 pp.

814 Osberg, Richard H. "Alliterative Lyrics in *Tottel's Miscellany*: The Persistence of a Medieval Style." *Studies in Philology* 76 (1979): 334–52.

815 Ostriker, Alicia. "The Three Modes in Tennyson's Prosody." *PMLA* 82 (1967): 273–84.

816 ———. *Vision and Verse in William Blake*. Madison: University of Wisconsin Press, 1965. 224 pp.

817 Owen, W. J. B. "The Theory of Metre." *Wordsworth as Critic*. Toronto: University of Toronto Press, 1969. Pp. 27–36.

818 Parrish, Stephen. "Wordsworth and Coleridge on Meter." *JEGP* 59 (1960): 41–49.

819 Pattison, Bruce. *Music and Poetry of the English Renaissance*. London: Methuen, 1948.

820 Pound, Ezra. "Treatise on Metre." *ABC of Reading*. New York: New Directions, 1934. Pp. 195–206.

821 Propst, Louise. *An Analytical Study of Shelley's Versification*. Iowa City: University of Iowa, 1933. 74 pp.

822 Pyle, Fitzroy. "Pyrrhic and Spondee." *Hermathena* 107 (1968): 49–74.

823 Pyre, J. F. A. *The Formation of Tennyson's Style*. Madison: University of Wisconsin Press, 1921. 249 pp.

824 Ramsay, Robert L. "Changes in Verse-Technic in the Sixteenth-Century English Drama." *American Journal of Philology* 31 (1910): 175–202.

825 Ransom, John Crowe. "Wanted: An Ontological Critic." *The New Criticism*. New York: New Directions, 1941; rpt. in Chatman and Levin, eds. [9], pp. 269–82.

826 Ratcliffe, Stephen. *Campion: On Song*. Boston: Routledge & Kegan Paul, 1981. 200 pp.

❖ Richards, I. A. [235–36].

827 Richardson, Leon J. "Repetition and Rhythm in Vergil and Shakespeare." *University of California Chronicle* 32 (1930): 177–82.

828 Schleiner, Louise. *The Living Lyre in English Verse from Elizabeth through the Restoration*. Columbia: University of Missouri Press, 1984. 224 pp.

829 Selden, R. "Roughness in Satire from Horace to Dryden." *Modern Language Review* 66 (1971): 264–71.

830 Smith, Barbara Herrnstein. *Poetic Closure: A Study of How Poems End*. Chicago: University of Chicago Press, 1968. 289 pp.

❖ Smith, Chard Powers [81].

831 Smith, G. Gregory, ed. *Elizabethan Critical Essays*. 2 vols. Oxford: Clarendon Press, 1904; rpt. 1971.

The standard texts of the Renaissance English prosodists.

832 Stanford, Donald E. "The Experimentalist Poet." *In the Classic Mode: The Achievement of Robert Bridges*. Newark: University of Delaware Press, 1978. Pp. 80–125.

833 ———, ed. *The Selected Letters of Robert Bridges*. 2 vols. Cranbury, N.J.: Associated University Presses, 1983–84. 1039 pp.

834 Stein, Arnold. "Meter and Meaning in Donne's Verse." *Sewanee Review* 52 (1944): 288–301.

835 Stevens, John E. *Music and Poetry in the Early Tudor Court*. 2nd ed., rev. London: Methuen, 1979.

836 ———. *The Old Sound and the New*. Cambridge: Cambridge University Press, 1982. 24 pp.

837 Stewart, George R., Jr. "The Iambic-Trochaic Theory in Relation to Musical Notation." *JEGP* 24 (1925): 61–71.

838 Taglicht, Josef. "Phonology, Scansion, Metre." *Proceedings of the Conference Held at Tel Aviv University, December 1968*. Tel Aviv: Association of University Teachers of English, 1969. Pp. 37–49.

839 Tsur, Reuven. "Articulateness and Requiredness in Iambic Verse." *Style* 6 (1972): 123–48.

840 Wells, Rulon. [Comments on Meter.] In Sebeok, ed. [57], pp. 197–200.

❖ Wesling, Donald [554].

❖ Winn, James A. [61].

841 Winters, Yvor. "The Influence of Meter on Poetic Convention." *Primitivism and Decadence: A Study in American Experimental Poetry*. New York: Arrow Editions, 1937; rpt. in his *In Defense of Reason*. Chicago: Swallow Press, 1947. Pp. 103–50.

842 Wode, Henning. "Linguistische Grundlagen verslicher Strukturen im Englischen." *Folia Linguistica* 4 (1970): 372–92.

843 Yeats, William Butler. "A General Introduction for My Work" (1937). Rpt. in his *Essays and Introductions*. New York: Macmillan, 1961. Pp. 509–30.

Old English

844 Bessinger, Jess B., Jr. "The Sutton Hoo Harp Replica and Old English Musical Verse." *Old English Poetry: Fifteen Essays*. Ed. Robert P. Creed. Providence: Brown University Press, 1967. Pp. 3–26.

845 Bliss, A. J. "The Appreciation of Old English Metre." *English and Medieval Studies Presented to J. R. R. Tolkien*. Ed. Norman Davis and C. L. Wrenn. London: Allen & Unwin, 1962. Pp. 27–40.

846 ———. *The Meter of "Beowulf."* 2nd ed. Oxford: Basil Blackwell, 1967. 170 pp.

❖ Brogan, T. V. F. [2], part 2, sec. 1 (J).

847 Burchfield, R. W. "The Prosodic Terminology of Anglo-Saxon Scholars." *Old English Studies in Honour of John C. Pope*. Ed. Robert B. Burlin and Edward B. Irving, Jr. Toronto: University of Toronto Press, 1974. Pp. 171–202.

848 Cable, Thomas. *The Meter and Melody of "Beowulf."* Urbana: University of Illinois Press, 1974. 122 pp.

849 Chase, Colin, ed. *The Dating of Beowulf*. Toronto: University of Toronto Press, 1981.

850 Creed, Robert P. "On the Possibility of Criticizing Old English Poetry." *Texas Studies in Literature and Language* 3 (1961): 97–106.

851 Foley, John Miles. "Hybrid Prosody and Single Half-Lines in Old English and Serbo-Croatian Poetry." *Neophilologus* 64 (1980): 284–89.

852 Fakundiny, Lydia. "The Art of Old English Verse Composition." *Review of English Studies*, n.s. 21 (1970): 129–43, 257–66.

853 Fowler, Roger. "*The Rhythm of Beowulf*—A Review." *Anglia* 87 (1969): 444–49; rpt. in his *The Language of Literature* [792], pp. 178–83.

854 Greg, W. W. "The 'Five Types' in Anglo-Saxon Verse." *Modern Language Review* 20 (1925): 12–17.

855 Gummere, Francis B. "The Translation of *Beowulf,* and the Relations of Ancient and Modern English Verse." *American Journal of Philology* 7 (1886): 46–78.

856 Kaluza, Max. *Der altenglische Verse: Eine metrische Untersuchung*. Berlin, 1894.

857 Kendall, C. B. "The Metrical Grammar of *Beowulf:* Displacement." *Speculum* 58 (1983): 1–30.

858 Kurylowicz, Jerzy. "Linguistic Fundamentals of the Meter of *Beowulf.*" *Linguistic and Literary Studies in Honor of Archibald A. Hill.* Ed. M. A. Jazayery et al. 4 vols. The Hague: Mouton, 1979. Vol. 4, pp. 111–19.

859 Le Page, R. B. "A Rhythmical Framework for the Five Types." *English and German Studies* 6 (1957): 92–103.

860 Lewis, C. S. "The Alliterative Metre" (1935); rpt. in his *Rehabilitations.* Oxford: Oxford University Press, 1939. Pp. 117–32.

861 Pope, John C. *The Rhythm of Beowulf.* Rev. ed. New Haven: Yale University Press, 1966. 409 pp.

862 Quirk, Randolph. "Poetic Language and Old English Metre." *Early English and Norse Studies.* Ed. Arthur Brown and Peter Foote. London: Methuen, 1963. Pp. 150–71.

863 Renoir, Alain, and Ann Hernandez, eds. *Approaches to Beowulfian Scansion.* Berkeley: Old English Colloquium, Department of English, University of California, 1982.

Introduction, four essays, and bibliography.

864 Rieger, Max. "Die alt- und angelsächsische Verskunst." *Zeitschrift für deutsches Altertum und deutsche Literatur* (1876): 1–64.

865 Russom, Geoffrey. *Old English Meter and Linguistic Theory.* Cambridge: Cambridge University Press, 1987. 178 pp.

❖ Sievers, Eduard [1251].

866 Taglicht, Josef. "*Beowulf* and Old English Verse Rhythm." *Review of English Studies,* n.s. 12 (1961): 341–51.

867 Wrenn, C. L. *A Study of Old English Literature.* London: Harrap, 1967; rpt. 1975. Chaps. 3–4.

MIDDLE ENGLISH

868 Bateson, F. W. "Could Chaucer Spell?" *Essays in Criticism* 25 (1975): 2–24.

869 Baugh, Albert C. "Improvisation in the Middle English Romance." *Proceedings of the American Philosophical Association* 103 (1959): 418–54.

870 Baum, Paull F. *Chaucer's Verse.* Durham: Duke University Press, 1961. 144 pp.

871 Blake, N. F. "Rhythmical Alliteration." *Modern Philology* 67 (1969): 118–24.

872 Borroff, Marie. *"Sir Gawain and the Green Knight": A Stylistic and Metrical Study*. New Haven: Yale University Press, 1962; rpt. Hamden, Conn.: Archon, 1973.

873 Brink, Bernhard Ten. *Chaucers Sprache und Verskunst*. Strassburg, 1884; 2nd ed. trans. by M. B. Smith as *The Language and Meter of Chaucer*. London: Macmillan, 1901.

❖ Brogan, T. V. F. [2], part 2, sec. 2 (K).

❖ Brook, G. L., ed. [492].

874 Dobson, E. J., and F. Ll. Harrison, eds. *Medieval English Songs*. New York: Cambridge University Press, 1979. 331 pp.

875 Donaldson, E. Talbot. "Chaucer's Final -*E*." *PMLA* 63 (1948): 1101–24.

❖ Dürmüller, Urs [464].

876 Duggan, Hoyt. "The Shape of the B-Verse in Middle English Alliterative Poetry." *Speculum* 61 (1986): 564–92.

877 Eliason, Norman E. *The Language of Chaucer's Poetry: An Appraisal of the Verse, Style, and Structure*. Copenhagen: Rosenkilde & Bagger, 1972.

❖ Ellis, Alexander J. [940].

878 Everett, Dorothy. *Essays on Middle English Literature*. Ed. Patricia Kean. Oxford: Clarendon Press, 1955. 179 pp.

879 Friedlander, Carolynn V. "Early Middle English Alliterative Verse." *Modern Philology* 76 (1978–79): 219–30.

880 Gaylord, Alan T. "Scanning the Prosodists: An Essay in Metacriticism." *Chaucer Review* 11 (1976): 22–82.

881 Gilbert, Dorothy. "The Rude Sweetness: A Study of Chaucer's Prosody and of Its Examiners." *DAI* 37, 1A (1976): 288 (California).

❖ Greene, Richard Leighton [350].

❖ Hammond, Eleanor P. [760].

❖ Honour, Margaret C. [774].

882 Ito, Masayoshi. *John Gower, the Medieval Poet*. Tokyo: Shinozaki Shorin, 1976. 309 pp.

883 Kittredge, George Lyman. "Metrical Chapter." *Observations on the Language of Chaucer's "Troilus."* London, 1891. Pp. 346–421.

884 Lawton, David A. "Gaytryge's Sermons, *Dictamen*, and Middle English Alliterative Verse." *Modern Philology* 76 (1978–79): 329–43.

885 ———, ed. *Middle English Alliterative Poetry and Its Literary Background*. Woodbridge, Eng.: D. S. Brewer, 1982.

886 Lewis, C. S. "The Fifteenth-Century Heroic Line." *Essays and Studies* 24 (1938): 28–41; rpt. in his *Selected Literary Essays* [807], pp. 45–57.

887 Lounsbury, Thomas R. *Studies in Chaucer, His Life and Writings*. 3 vols. New York, 1892.

888 Luick, Karl. "Englische Metrik: Geschichte der heimischen Versarten." In Paul, ed. [1180], pp. 141–80.

889 McIntosh, Angus. "Early Middle English Alliterative Verse." In Lawton, ed. [885], pp. 20–33, 129–31.

890 McNary, Sarah J. *Studies in Layamon's Verse*. Baltimore, 1904. 36 pp.

891 Manzalaoui, Malmoud. "Lydgate and English Prosody." *Cairo Studies in English*. Ed. Magdi Wahba. Cairo, 1960. Pp. 87–104.

892 Mustanoja, Tauno F. "Chaucer's Prosody." *Companion to Chaucer Studies*. Ed. Beryl Rowland. 2nd ed., rev. Oxford: Oxford University Press, 1979. Pp. 65–94.

893 Oakden, James P. *Alliterative Poetry in Middle English*. 2 vols. Manchester: Manchester University Press, 1930, 1935; rpt. Hamden, Conn.: Archon, 1968. 217 + 403 pp.

❖ Oliver, Raymond [508].

894 Osberg, Richard H. "Alliterative Lyrics and Thirteenth-Century Devotional Prose." *JEGP* 76 (1977): 40–54.

❖ ———. [814].

895 Pyle, Fitzroy. "Chaucer's Prosody." *Medium Ævum* 42 (1973): 47–56.

896 ———. "The Pedigree of Lydgate's Heroic Line, with a Note on His Use of the Line-types." *Hermathena*, no. 50 (1937): 26–59.

❖ Quinn, William, and Audley S. Hall [317].

897 Salter, Elizabeth. "Alliterative Modes and Affiliations in the Fourteenth Century." *Neuphilologische Mitteilungen* 79 (1978): 25–35.

❖ Schipper, Jakob [768].

898 ———. "Englische Metrik: Fremde Metra." In Paul, ed. [1180], pp. 181–240.

899 Skeat, W. W., ed. *The Complete Works of Geoffrey Chaucer*. 6 vols. Oxford: Oxford University Press, 1894. Vol. 6.

❖ Stevens, John [58].

900 Stobie, M. M. R. "The Influence of Morphology on Middle English Alliterative Poetry." *JEGP* 39 (1940): 319–36.

901 Turville-Petre, Joan. "The Metre of *Sir Gawain and the Green Knight*." *English Studies* 57 (1976): 310–28.

902 Turville-Petre, Thorlac. *The Alliterative Revival*. Cambridge: D. S. Brewer, 1977. 152 pp.

903 Tyrwhitt, Thomas. *An Essay on the Language and Versification of Chaucer.* Vol. 4 of his ed. of *The Canterbury Tales of Chaucer.* 5 vols. London, 1775; rpt. New York: AMS, 1978.

904 West, Henry S. *The Versification of "King Horn."* Baltimore, 1907. 92 pp.

905 Wimsatt, James I. *Chaucer and the Poems of "Ch" in University of Pennsylvania MS French 15.* Cambridge: D. S. Brewer, 1982. 136 pp.

ANGLO-NORMAN

906 Johnston, R. C. *The Versification of Jordan Fantosme.* Oxford: Basil Blackwell, 1974. 34 pp.

907 ———. "Matthew Paris, Jordan Fantosme, and Anglo-Norman Versification." *Mélanges de langue et littérature françaises.* Rennes: Université de Haute-Bretagne, 1980. Pp. 165–75.

908 ———, ed. *Jordan Fantosme's Chronicle.* Oxford: Clarendon Press, 1981.

See the introduction and appendixes.

909 Legge, M. Dominica. *Anglo-Norman Literature and Its Background.* Oxford: Clarendon Press, 1963. 389 pp.

910 Pyle, Fitzroy. "The Place of Anglo-Norman in the History of English Versification." *Hermathena,* no. 49 (1935): 22–42.

911 Wind, B. H. "Quelques Remarques sur la versification de Thomas." *Neophilologus* 33 (1949): 85–95.

MODERN ENGLISH

Meters

Ballad and Hymn Meter

912 Boswell, George W. "Reciprocal Controls Exerted by Ballad Texts and Tunes." *Journal of American Folklore* 80 (1967): 169–74.

913 ———. "Stanza Form and Music-Imposed Scansion in Southern Ballads." *Southern Folklore Quarterly* 31 (1967): 320–31.

914 Bronson, Bertrand H. *The Ballad as Song.* Berkeley and Los Angeles: University of California Press, 1969. 324 pp.

915 ———. *The Singing Tradition of Child's Popular Ballads.* Princeton: Princeton University Press, 1976.

916 ———. "Traditional Ballads Musically Considered." *Critical Inquiry* 2 (1975): 29–42.

917 Calendar, Carl E. "Metrical Translations of the Psalms in France and England, 1530–1650." *DAI* 33, 12A (1973): 6863 (Oregon).

918 Coffin, Tristram P. "Remarks Preliminary to a Study of Ballad Meter and Ballad Singing." *Journal of American Folklore* 78 (1965): 149–53.

919 Freer, Coburn. *Music For a King: George Herbert's Style and the Metrical Psalms.* Baltimore: Johns Hopkins University Press, 1972. 252 pp.

920 Gerould, Gordon H. *The Ballad of Tradition.* Cambridge, Mass.: Harvard University Press, 1932; rpt. New York: Gordian, 1974. 311 pp. Chaps. 4, 8.

921 Hendren, J. W. *A Study of Ballad Rhythm, with Special Reference to Ballad Music.* Princeton: Princeton University Press, 1936. 177 pp.

922 Huttar, Charles A. "English Metrical Paraphrases of the Psalms, 1500–1640." *DAI* 17, 3A (1957): 631 (Northwestern).

923 Lovegrove, Glenda S. "Introduction to Hymn Meter and the Development of Prosodic Regularity in Sixteenth-Century Poetry." Ph.D. diss., Harvard University, 1974.

❖ Malof, Joseph [1052].

924 Smith, Hallet. "English Metrical Psalms in the Sixteenth Century and Their Literary Significance." *Huntington Library Quarterly* 9 (1946): 249–71.

925 Stewart, George R., Jr. "The Meter of the Popular Ballad." *PMLA* 40 (1925): 933–62.

926 ———. "A Method toward the Study of Dipodic Verse." *PMLA* 39 (1924): 979–89.

927 ———. *Modern Metrical Technique as Illustrated by Ballad Meter (1700–1920).* New York, 1922. 120 pp.

Iambic Pentameter

928 Adler, Jacob H. *The Reach of Art: A Study in the Prosody of Pope.* Gainesville: University of Florida Press, 1964.

929 Amis, George T. "The Structure of the Augustan Couplet." *Genre* 9 (1976): 37–58.

930 Baldi, Sergio. *La Poesia di Sir Thomas Wyatt.* Florence: Le Monnier, 1953.

931 Baldwin, T. W. "Upper Grammar School: Shakspere's Exercise of Versifying." *William Shakspere's Small Latine and Lesse Greeke.* 2 vols. Urbana: University of Illinois Press, 1944. Vol. 2, pp. 380–416.

932 Beum, Robert. "So Much Gravity and Ease." *Language and Style in Milton.* Ed. Ronald D. Emma and John T. Shawcross. New York: Ungar, 1967. Pp. 333–68.

933 Bridges, Robert. *Milton's Prosody: with a chapter on Accentual Verse & Notes.* Rev. ed. Oxford: Clarendon Press, 1921; rpt. Oxford: Oxford University Press, 1967. 119 pp.

934 Brown, Wallace Cable. *The Triumph of Form: A Study of the Later Masters of the Heroic Couplet.* Chapel Hill: University of North Carolina Press, 1948.

935 Chambers, E. K. "Appendix H: Metrical Tables." *William Shakespeare: A Study of Facts and Problems.* 2 vols. Oxford: Clarendon Press, 1930. Vol. 2, pp. 397–408.

936 Clark, Arthur Melville. "Milton and the Renaissance Revolt against Rhyme." In his *Studies in Literary Modes.* Edinburgh: Oliver & Boyd, 1946. Pp. 105–41.

937 Coulter, Mary D. "The English Iambic Pentameter in Nondramatic and Dramatic Verse, 1590–1640." *DAI* 43, 3A (1982): 796 (George Washington). 374 pp.

938 Cayley, C. B. "The Pedigree of the English Heroic Verse." *Transactions of the Philological Society,* 1867, pp. 43–54.

939 Diekhoff, John S. "Milton's Prosody in the Poems of the Trinity Manuscript." *PMLA* 54 (1939): 153–83.

940 Ellis, Alexander J. *On Early English Pronunciation.* 5 pts. London: Early English Text Society, 1869–89.

      Pt. 1, chap. 4 on Chaucer; pt. 3, chap. 7 on Shakespeare.

941 Eliot, T. S. "Shakespeares Verskunst." *Der Monat* 2 (1950): 198–207.

942 Evans, Robert O. "Some Aspects of Wyatt's Metrical Technique." *JEGP* 53 (1954): 197–213.

943 Fleay, F. G. *Shakespeare Manual.* 2nd ed. London: n.p., 1878; rpt. New York: AMS, 1970.

944 Fowler, Roger. "Three Blank Verse Textures" in his *The Languages of Literature* [792], pp. 184–99.

945 Franz, Wilhelm. *Shakespeare's Blankvers, mit Nachträgen zu des Verfasser's Shakespeare-Grammatik.* 2nd ed. Tübingen: Verlag des englischen Seminars in Tübingen, 1935. 104 pp.

946 Hardison, O. B., Jr. "Blank Verse Before Milton." *Studies in Philology* 81 (1984): 253–74.

947 Havens, Raymond D. *The Influence of Milton on English Poetry.* Cambridge, Mass.: Harvard University Press, 1922.

948 Hemphill, George. "Dryden's Heroic Line." *PMLA* 72 (1957): 863–79.

949 Johnson, Lee M. *Wordsworth's Metaphysical Poetry: Geometry, Nature, and Form.* Toronto: University of Toronto Press, 1982. 241 pp.

950 Jones, John A. *Pope's Couplet Art*. Athens: Ohio State University Press, 1969. 217 pp.

951 Kökeritz, Helge. "Elizabethan Prosody and Historical Phonology." *Annales Academiae Regiae Scientiarum Upsaliensis* 5 (1961): 79–102.

952 König, Goswin. *Der Vers in Shaksperes Dramen*. Strassburg: Trübner, 1888. 138 pp.

953 Morton, Edward P. *The Technique of English Nondramatic Blank Verse*. Chicago: R. R. Donnelly, 1910; rpt. Norwood, Pa.: Norwood Editions, 1975.

954 Oras, Ants. *Blank Verse and Chronology in Milton*. Gainesville: University of Florida Press, 1966. 81 pp.

955 Piper, William Bowman. *Evaluating Shakespeare's Sonnets*. Houston: Rice University Press, 1979.

956 Prince, F. T. *The Italian Element in Milton's Verse*. Oxford: Clarendon Press, 1954. 183 pp.

957 Ramsey, Paul. "The Metrical Rules of the Sonnets." *The Fickle Glass: A Study of Shakespeare's Sonnets*. New York: AMS, 1979. Pp. 65–98.

958 Rudenstein, Neil L. "Style as Convention." *Sidney's Poetic Development*. Cambridge, Mass.: Harvard University Press, 1967. Pp. 75–105.

959 Schoenbaum, Samuel. *Internal Evidence and the Authorship of Shakespeare's Plays*. Evanston, Ill.: Northwestern University Press, 1966.

960 Shannon, George P. "Nicholas Grimald's Heroic Couplet and the Latin Elegiac Distich." *PMLA* 45 (1930): 532–42.

961 Simpson, Percy. "Shakespeare's Versification: A Study of Development." *Studies in Elizabethan Drama*. Oxford: Clarendon Press, 1955. Pp. 64–88.

962 Sipe, Dorothy L. *Shakespeare's Metrics*. New Haven: Yale University Press, 1968. 266 pp.

963 Smart, G. K. "English Non-dramatic Blank Verse in the Sixteenth Century." *Anglia* 61 (1937): 370–97.

964 Smith, Hallet. "The Art of Sir Thomas Wyatt." *Huntington Library Quarterly* 9 (1946): 323–55.

965 Southall, Raymond. *The Courtly Makers: An Essay on the Poetry of Wyatt and His Contemporaries*. Oxford: Basil Blackwell, 1964.

966 Sprott, S. Ernest. *Milton's Art of Prosody*. Oxford: Basil Blackwell, 1953. 147 pp.

967 Stein, Arnold. "Donne and the Couplet." *PMLA* 57 (1942): 676–96.

968 ———. "Structures of Sound in Donne's Verse." *Kenyon Review* 13 (1951): 20–36, 256–78.

969 Suhamy, Henri. *Le Vers de Shakespeare*. Paris: Didier, 1984. 784 pp.

970 Symonds, John Addington. *Blank Verse*. London, 1895.

971 Tarlinskaja, M[arina] G. "Evolution of Shakespeare's Metrical Style." *Poetics* 12 1983): 567–87.

972 ———. *Shakespeare's Verse: Iambic Pentameter and the Poet's Idiosyncrasies*. New York: Peter Lang, 1987. 383 pp.

973 Wallerstein, Ruth. "The Development of the Rhetoric and Metre of the Heroic Couplet, Especially in 1625–1645." *PMLA* 50 (1935): 166–209.

974 Weismiller, Edward R. "Blank Verse." *A Milton Encyclopedia*. Ed. William B. Hunter, Jr. 8 vols. Lewisburg, Pa.: Bucknell University Press, 1978–80. Vol. 1, pp. 179–92.

975 ———. "The 'Dry' and 'Rugged' Verse." *The Lyric and Dramatic Milton*. Ed. Joseph H. Summers. New York: Columbia University Press, 1965. Pp. 115–52.

976 ———. "Studies of Style and Verse Form in *Paradise Regained*." *A Variorum Commentary on the Poems of John Milton*. Ed. Merritt Y. Hughes. New York: Columbia University Press, 1975. Vol. 4, pp. 253–364.

977 ———. "Studies of Verse Form in the Minor English Poems." In the *Variorum Commentary* [976]. Vol. 2, pp. 1007–87.

978 Wentersdorf, Karl. "Shakespearean Chronology and the Metrical Tests." *Shakespeare-Studien: Festschrift für Heinrich Mutschmann*. Ed. Walther Fischer and Karl Wentersdorf. Marburg: N. G. Elwert, 1951. Pp. 161–93.

979 Whiteley, M. "Verse and Its Feet." *Review of English Studies,* n.s. 9 (1958): 268–78.

980 Williamson, George. "The Rhetorical Pattern of Neo-Classical Wit." *Modern Philology* 33 (1935): 55–81.

981 Wright, George T. *Shakespeare's Metrical Art*. Berkeley and Los Angeles: University of California Press, 1988. 349 pp.

982 ———. "Wyatt's Decasyllabic Line." *Studies in Philology* 82 (1985): 129–56.

Triple Meters

983 Breen, Ann T. "A Survey of the Development of Poetry Written in Trisyllic Metres to 1830, Approximately." Ph.D. diss., National University of Ireland, 1965.

❖ Hascall, Dudley L. [1082].

Sprung Rhythm

984 Gardner, W. H. *Gerard Manley Hopkins (1844–1889): A Study of Poetic Idiosyncrasy in Relation to Poetic Tradition*. 2 vols. London: Martin Secker & Warburg, 1948–49.

985 Holloway, Marcella M., Sister. *The Prosodic Theory of Gerard Manley Hopkins*. Washington, D.C.: Catholic University of America Press, 1947. 117 pp.

986 Hopkins, Gerard Manley. "Author's Preface." *The Poems of Gerard Manley Hopkins*. 4th rev. and enl. ed. Ed. W. H. Gardner and N. H. MacKenzie. London: Oxford University Press, 1967; rpt. 1970. Pp. 45–49.

987 House, Humphry, and Graham Storey, eds. *The Journals and Papers of Gerard Manley Hopkins*. London: Oxford University Press, 1959.

988 Ludwig, Hans-Werner. *Barbarous in Beauty: Studien zum Vers im G. M. Hopkins' Sonetten*. Munich: Wilhelm Fink, 1972. 396 pp.

989 Ong, Walter J., S.J. "Hopkins' Sprung Rhythm and the Life of English Poetry." *Immortal Diamond*. Ed. Norman Weyand. London: Sheed & Ward, 1949. Pp. 83–174.

990 Schneider, Elizabeth. *The Dragon in the Gate: Studies in the Poetry of G. M. Hopkins*. Berkeley and Los Angeles: University of California Press, 1968. Chaps. 3–4.

991 Ventre, Raymond J. "Gerard Manley Hopkins: Sprung Rhythm and Meaning." *DAI* 39, 10A (1979): 6151 (Brown).

❖ Wesling, Donald. "Sprung Rhythm and the Figure of Grammar." In Wesling [554], pp. 113–44.

Theories

Surveys

992 Barkas, Pallister A. *A Critique of Modern English Prosody (1880–1930)*. Halle: Max Niemeyer, 1934. 100 pp.

❖ Brogan, T. V. F. [2]. Introduction to chap. 6.

993 Chatman, Seymour, and Samuel R. Levin. "Linguistics and Literature." *Current Trends in Linguistics, X*. Ed. Thomas A. Sebeok. The Hague: Mouton, 1973. Pp. 250–94.

Reviews chiefly structural-linguistic work of the 1950s and 1960s.

994 Eaton, Richard B., Jr. "A History of American Prosody from Its Beginnings to 1880." *DAI* 28, 9A (1968): 3669 (North Carolina).

❖ Ern, Lothar [527].

995 Fussell, Paul, Jr. *Theory of Prosody in Eighteenth-Century England*. New London, Conn.: Connecticut College Monographs, 1954; rpt. Hamden, Conn.: Archon, 1966. 170 pp.

996 Meyers, Gerald W. "Modern Theories of Meter: A Critical Review." *DAI* 30, 9A (1970): 3912 (Michigan).

❖ Saintsbury, George [767].

997 Schelling, Felix E. *Poetic and Verse Criticism of the Reign of Elizabeth*. Philadelphia: University of Pennsylvania Press, 1892. 97 pp.

❖ Schipper, Jakob [769].

998 Thiesmeyer, John E. "Prosodic Theory: A Critique and Some Proposals." *DAI* 35, 2A (1974): 1064 (Cornell).

Quantitative

999 Adams, Stephen J. "Pound's Quantities and 'Absolute Rhythm.' " *Essays in Literature* 4 (1977): 95–109.

1000 Arnold, Matthew. *Three Lectures on Translating Homer*. London: Longmans, 1861.

❖ Attridge, Derek [733].

1001 Aylward, Kevin H. "Milton's Latin Versification: The Hexameter." *DAI* 27, 4A (1966): 1331 (Columbia).

1002 Bridges, Robert. Introduction. *Ibant Obscuri: An Experiment in the Classical Hexameter*. Oxford: Clarendon Press, 1916.

1003 Dilligan, Robert J. "Ibant Obscuri: Robert Bridges' Experiment in English Quantitative Verse." *Style* 6 (1972): 38–65.

❖ Dunn, Catherine M. [739].

❖ Elze, Karl [740].

1004 Fenyo, Jane K. "Grammar and Music in Thomas Campion's *Observations in the Art of English Poesie*." *Studies in the Renaissance* 17 (1970): 46–72.

1005 Hendrickson, G. L. "Elizabethan Quantitative Hexameters." *Philological Quarterly* 28 (1949): 237–60.

1006 McKerrow, R. B. "The Use of So-Called Classical Metres in Elizabethan Verse." *Modern Language Quarterly* 4 (1901): 172–80; 5 (1902): 5–13, 148–49.

1007 Omond, T. S. *English Hexameter Verse*. Edinburgh: David Douglas, 1897. 48 pp.

❖ Park, Ben A. [744].

1008 Ringler, William. "Master Drant's Rules." *Philological Quarterly* 29 (1950): 70–74.

1009 Schuman, Sharon. "Sixteenth-Century English Quantitative Verse: Its Ends, Means, and Products." *Modern Philology* 74 (1977): 335–49.

1010 Southey, Robert. Preface. *A Vision of Judgment*. London, 1821.

1011 Standop, Ewald. "Zur Beurteilung der Elisabethanischen Hexameter." *Studien zur englischen und amerikanischen Sprache und Literatur*. Ed. Paul G. Buchloh et al. Neumünster: Wacholtz, 1974. Pp. 350–62.

1012 Stone, William Johnson. *On the Use of Classical Metres in English*. London, 1898; 2nd ed. added to the 1901 edition of Robert Bridges' *Milton's Prosody* [933].

Temporal

1013 Alden, R. M. *An Introduction to Poetry for Students of English Literature*. 2nd ed. New York: Henry Holt, 1937.

1014 Brown, Calvin S. "Can Musical Notation Help English Scansion?" *JAAC* 23 (1965): 329–34.

1015 Hollander, John. "The Music of Poetry." *JAAC* 15 (1956): 232–44.

1016 Lanier, Sidney. *The Science of English Verse*. New York: Charles Scribner's Sons, 1880; rpt. with editor's introduction in vol. 2 of the *Centennial Edition of the Works of Sidney Lanier*. Ed. Paull F. Baum. Baltimore: Johns Hopkins Press, 1945.

1017 Lightfoot, Marjorie J. "Numerical, Sequential, and Temporal Patterns in English Poetry." *Quarterly Journal of Speech* 57 (1971): 193–203.

1018 ———. "Temporal Prosody: Verse Feet, Measures, Time, Syllabic Distribution, and Isochronous Accent." *Language and Style* 7 (1974): 245–60.

1019 Mussulman, Joseph A. "A Descriptive System of Musical Prosody." *Centennial Review of Arts and Sciences* 9 (1965): 332–47.

1020 Omond, T. S. *A Study of Metre*. London: Grant Richards, 1903.

1021 Patmore, Coventry. "English Metrical Critics." *North British Review* 27 (1857): 127–61. Rev. as "Prefatory Study of English Metrical Law" in his *Amelia*. London, 1878. Ed. Sister Mary Augustine Roth. Washington, D.C.: Catholic University of America Press, 1961.

Includes bibliography.

1022 Perry, John O. "The Temporal Analysis of Poems." *British Journal of Aesthetics* 5 (1965): 227–45.

1023 Poe, Edgar Allan. "The Rationale of Verse." In the *Complete Works*. Ed. James A. Harrison. 17 vols. New York: Crowell, 1902. Vol. 14, pp. 209–65.

1024 Schramm, Wilbur Lang. *Approaches to a Science of English Verse*. Iowa City: The University, 1935. 82 pp.

1025 Scripture, E. W. *Grundzüge der englischen Verswissenschaft*. Marburg: N. G. Elwert, 1929. 98 pp.

1026 Smith, Egerton. *Principles of English Metre*. London: Oxford University Press, 1923. 326 pp.

1027 Steele, Joshua. *Prosodia Rationalis: or an Essay Toward Establishing the Melody and Measure of Speech*. London, 1779.

1028 Stewart, George R., Jr. *The Technique of English Verse*. New York: Holt, Rinehart & Winston, 1930; rpt. Port Washington, N.Y.: Kennikat, 1966. 235 pp.

1029 Sumera, Magdalena. "The Temporal Tradition in the Study of Verse Structure." *Linguistics* 62 (1970): 44–65.

❖ Taig, Thomas [244].

1030 Thomson, William. *The Rhythm of Speech*. Glasgow, 1923. 559 pp.

1031 Verrier, Paul. *Essai sur les principes de la métrique anglaise*. 3 vols. Paris: Libraire Universitaire, 1909–10.

1032 Wilson, Katharine M. *The Real Rhythm in English Poetry*. Aberdeen: Aberdeen University Press, 1929. 171 pp.

Accentual

1033 Abercrombie, Lascelles. *Principles of English Prosody*. London: Martin Secker, 1923. 155 pp.

1034 Attridge, Derek. *The Rhythms of English Poetry*. London: Longmans Group, 1982. 395 pp.

1035 Bailey, James. *Toward a Statistical Analysis of English Verse: The Iambic Tetrameter of Ten Poets*. Lisse: Peter de Ridder, 1975. 79 pp.

1036 Baum, Paull F. *The Principles of English Versification*. Cambridge, Mass.: Harvard University Press, 1922; rpt. Hamden, Conn.: Archon, 1969. 215 pp.

❖ Bridges, Robert [933].

1037 Bysshe, Edward. *The Art of English Poetry*. London, 1702; many subsequent editions.

1038 Culler, A. Dwight. "Edward Bysshe and the Poet's Handbook." *PMLA* 63 (1948): 858–85.

1039 Daniel, Samuel. *A Defense of Rhyme*. London, 1603.

1040 Diller, Hans-Jürgen. *Metrik und Verslehre*. Düsseldorf: Bagel, 1979.

❖ Ellis, Alexander J. [940].

1041 Fussell, Paul, Jr. *Poetic Meter and Poetic Form*. 2nd ed. New York: Random House, 1979. 188 pp.

1042 Gascoigne, George. "Certayne Notes of Instruction concerning the making of verse or ryme in English." In his *Posies*. London, 1575; rpt. in the *Complete Works*. Ed. John W. Cunliffe. Cambridge: Cambridge University Press, 1907–10.

1043 Gill, Alexander. *Logonomia Anglica*. London, 1619. Ed. Bror and Arvid Danielsson. Stockholm: Almqvist & Wiksell, 1972.

1044 Guest, Edwin. *A History of English Rhythms*. 2 vols. London, 1838; 2nd ed. edited by W. W. Skeat. London: George Bell, 1882.

1045 Gummere, Francis B. *A Handbook of Poetics for Students of English Verse*. 3rd ed. Boston: Ginn, 1890.

1046 Hamer, Enid. *The Metres of English Poetry*. London: Methuen, 1930. 334 pp.

1047 Jespersen, Otto. "Notes on Metre" (1900); rpt. in his *Linguistica: Selected Papers in English, French, and German*. Copenhagen: Levin & Munksgaard, 1933. Pp. 249–74; rpt. in Chatman and Levin, eds. [9], pp. 71–90.

1048 Johnson, Samuel. "Prosody." Final section of the "Grammar of the English Tongue" prefixed to the *Dictionary of the English Language*. London, 1755.

1049 ———. *The Rambler*. Nos. 86, 88, 90. London, 1751. Rpt. in the Yale Edition of the *Works of Samuel Johnson*. Ed. W. Jackson Bate and A. B. Straus. New Haven: Yale University Press, 1969. Vol. 4.

1050 Kames, Henry Home, Lord. *Elements of Criticism*. 3 vols. London, 1762; rpt. Hildesheim: Georg Olms, 1970. Vol. 2, chap. 18.

1051 McAuley, James. *Versification: A Short Introduction*. East Lansing: Michigan State University Press, 1966; rpt. 1987. 84 pp.

1052 Malof, Joseph. *A Manual of English Meters*. Bloomington: Indiana University Press, 1970; rpt. Westport, Conn.: Greenwood, 1978. 236 pp.

1053 Mayor, Joseph B. *Chapters on English Metre*. 2nd ed. Cambridge: Cambridge University Press, 1901; rpt. New York: AMS, 1969. 308 pp.

1054 Puttenham, George. *The Arte of English Poesie*. London, 1589. Ed. Gladys D. Willcock and Alice Walker. Cambridge: Cambridge University Press, 1936; rpt. 1970.

1055 Pyle, Fitzroy. "The Rhythm of the English Heroic Line: An Essay in Empirical Analysis." *Hermathena*, no. 53 (1939): 100–126.

1056 Saintsbury, George. *Historical Manual of English Prosody*. London: Macmillan, 1910; rpt. New York: Schocken, 1966. 340 pp.

1057 Say, Samuel. *Poems on Several Occasions: and Two Critical Essays, viz. The First, on the Harmony, Variety, and Power of Numbers, whether in Prose or Verse. The Second, On the Numbers of "Paradise Lost."* London, 1745.

❖ Schipper, Jakob [768–69].

1058 Shapiro, Karl, and Robert Beum. *A Prosody Handbook*. New York: Harper & Row, 1965. 214 pp.

1059 Spiegel, Glenn S. "Perfecting English Meter: Sixteenth-Century Criticism and Practice." *JEGP* 79 (1980): 192–209.

❖ Tarlinskaja, M. G. [770].

1060 Wimsatt, W. K., Jr., and Monroe C. Beardsley. "The Concept of Meter: An Exercise in Abstraction." *PMLA* 74 (1959): 585–98.

1061 Young, George, Sir. *An English Prosody on Inductive Lines*. Cambridge: Cambridge University Press, 1928. 279 pp.

Structural Linguistic

1062 Chatman, Seymour. "Comparing Metrical Styles." In Sebeok, ed. [57], pp. 149–72; rpt. in Chatman and Levin, eds. [9], pp. 132–55.

1063 ———. *A Theory of Meter*. The Hague: Mouton, 1965. 229 pp.

1064 "English Verse and What It Sounds Like." *Kenyon Review* 18 (1956): 411–77.

     Two traditional critics confront two structural linguists in this symposium.

1065 Epstein, Edmund L., and Terence Hawkes. *Linguistics and English Prosody*. Buffalo: University of Buffalo Department of Anthropology, 1959. 50 pp.

1066 Fowler, Roger. "Structural Metrics." *Linguistics* 27 (1966): 49–64; rpt. in his *The Languages of Literature* [792], pp. 124–40.

1067 Hewitt, Elizabeth K. "Prosody: A Structuralist Approach." *Style* 6 (1972): 229–59.

1068 Stein, Arnold. "George Herbert's Prosody." *Language and Style* 1 (1968): 1–38.

1069 Whitehall, Harold. "From Linguistics to Criticism." *Kenyon Review* 13 (1951): 710–14.

Generative Linguistic

1070 Beaver, Joseph C. "Contrastive Stress and Metered Verse." *Language and Style* 2 (1969): 257–71.

1071 ———. "Generative Metrics: The Present Outlook." *Poetics* 12 (1974): 7–28.

1072 ———. "The Rules of Stress in English Verse." *Language* 47 (1971): 586–614.

1073 Bjorklund, Beth. *A Study in Comparative Prosody: English and German Iambic Pentameter*. Stuttgart: Heinz, 1978. 494 pp.

1074 Cable, Thomas. "Recent Developments in Metrics." *Style* 10 (1976): 313–28.

1075 Devine, A. M., and L. D. Stephens. "The Abstractness of Metrical Patterns: Generative Metrics and Explicit Traditional Metrics." *Poetics*, n.s. 4, no. 4 (1975): 411–29.

1076 Dilligan, Robert J., and Karen Lynn. "Computers and the History of Prosody." *College English* 34 (1973): 1103–23.

1077 Fowler, Rowena. "Metrics and the Transformational-Generative Model." *Lingua* 38 (1976): 21–36.

1078 Freeman, Donald C. "On the Primes of Metrical Style." *Language and Style* 1 (1968): 63–101.

1079 Halle, Morris, and Samuel J. Keyser. "Chaucer and the Study of Prosody." *College English* 28 (1966): 187–219.

1080 ———. *English Stress: Its Form, Its Growth, Its Role in Verse.* New York: Harper & Row, 1971. 186 pp.

1081 ———. "Illustration and Defense of a Theory of the Iambic Pentameter." *College English* 33 (1971): 154–76.

1082 Hascall, Dudley L. "Triple Meters in English Verse." *Poetics* 12 (1974): 49–772.

1083 ———. "Trochaic Meter." *College English* 33 (1971): 217–26.

1084 Hayes, Bruce. "A Grid-based Theory of English Meter." *Linguistic Inquiry* 14 (1983): 357–93.

1085 Kiparsky, Paul. "The Rhythmic Structure of English Verse." *Linguistic Inquiry* 8 (1977): 189–247.

1086 Klein, Wolfgang. "Critical Remarks on Generative Metrics." *Poetics* 12 (1974): 29–48.

1087 Levin, Samuel R. "A Revision of the Halle-Keyser Metrical Theory." *Language* 49 (1973): 606 11.

1088 Lord, John. B., Sr. "Some Solved and Some Unsolved Problems in Prosody." *Style* 13 (1979): 311–33.

1089 Magnuson, Karl, and Frank G. Ryder. "Second Thoughts on English Prosody." *College English* 33 (1971): 189–216.

1090 ———. "The Study of English Prosody: An Alternative Proposal." *College English* 31 (1970): 789–820.

1091 Newton, Robert P. "Trochaic and Iambic." *Language and Style* 8 (1975): 127–56.

1092 Sledd, James. "Old English Prosody: A Demurrer." *College English* 31 (1969): 71–74.

1093 Standop, Ewald. "Metric Theory Gone Astray: A Critique of the Halle-Keyser Theory." *Language and Style* 8 (1975): 60–77.

1094 Tsur, Reuven. *A Perception-oriented Theory of Metre.* Tel Aviv: Porter Institute for Poetics, Tel Aviv University, 1977. 244 pp.

1095 Wimsatt, W. K., Jr. "The Rule and the Norm: Halle and Keyser on Chaucer's Meter." *College English* 31 (1970): 774–88.

1096 Youmans, Gilbert. "Generative Tests for Generative Meter." *Language* 59 (1983): 67–92.

FRENCH

BIBLIOGRAPHIES

❖ Brogan, T. V. F. [2], pp. 646–60.

1097 *French XX Bibliography: Critical and Bibliographical References for the Study of French Literature Since 1885.* New York: French Institute, 1949–.

First volume covers 1940–48.

1098 Klapp, Otto, ed. *Bibliographie der französischen Literaturwissenschaft.* Frankfurt am Main: Klostermann, 1960–.

Coverage begins 1956. S.v. "Généralities: Poésie."

1099 Le Hir, Yves. *Esthétique et structure du vers français, après les théoreticiens du XVIe siècle à nos jours.* Paris: Presses Universitaires de France, 1956. 275 pp.

A historical survey of principal works on French prosody from 1500 to 1956, organized chronologically, with a chapter on each century and a long post-script. The chapter on the twentieth century covers a third of the book. Important works often merit long discussion, but a large number of second-ary and periodical works in this century are also noticed.

1100 Mazaleyrat, Jean. *Pour une étude rythmique du vers français moderne: Notes bibliographiques.* Paris: M. J. Minard/Lettres modernes, 1963. 125 pp.

1101 Thieme, Hugo P. *Essai sur l'histoire du vers français.* Paris: Honoré Champion, 1916; rpt. New York: Burt Franklin, 1971. 432 pp.

The standard bibliography of French works on prosody from 1332 to 1914. The works are discussed first in chapters on the various topics, followed by the bibliography itself, which is set forth in chronological order (usefully) but (irritatingly) separated into two parts, books then articles, followed by indexes. Note that "Bibliographie" is also one of the sections in the index (364–65) and is discussed in the text (16–20): forty-nine other bibliographic items are cited. Some few items from 1916 to 1932 are added by Thieme to the end of the lists on "Versification, arts poétiques," in his *Bibliographie de la littérature française de 1800 à 1930,* vol. 3, *La Civilisation* (1933), pp. 51–71. Selective citations for works after 1932 are given in Brogan [2], appendix.

ENCYCLOPEDIAS, DICTIONARIES

1102 Gröber, Gustav, ed. *Grundriss der romanischen Philologie.* 2 vols. in 4. Strass-burg: K. J. Trubner, 1888–1902.

1103 Jauss, Hans Robert, and Erich Köhler, eds. *Grundriss der romanischen Litera-turen des Mittelalters.* 9 vols. projected. Heidelberg: Carl Winter, 1968–.

1104 Morier, Henri. *Dictionnaire de poétique et de rhétorique.* 3rd ed. Paris: Presses Universitaires de France, 1981. 1262 pp.

HISTORIES

See also the studies of the emergence of Romance verse from Latin, which are listed on p. 55.

1105 Lote, Georges. *Histoire du vers français.* 3 vols. Paris: Boivan, 1949–56.

Title page says "Part One"; consequently these volumes focus almost entirely on the Middle Ages. Part Two never published.

1106 Kastner, L. E. *A History of French Versification.* Oxford: Clarendon Press, 1903. 312 pp.

Not primarily historical, in fact.

1107 Patterson, Warner Forrest. *Three Centuries of French Poetic Theory: A Critical History of the Chief Arts of Poetry in France (1328-1630).* 2 vols. Ann Arbor: University of Michigan Press, 1935.

1108 Verrier, Paul. *Le Vers français.* 3 vols. Paris: Didier, 1931–32.

STANZA INDEXES

1109 Frank, István. *Répertoire métrique de la poésie des troubadours.* 2 vols. Vol. 1: *Introduction et répertoire.* Vol. 2: *Répertoire (suite) et index bibliographique.* Paris: Champion, 1953, 1957; rpt. 1966. 195 + 234 pp.

1110 Martinon, Philippe. *Les Strophes: Etude historique et critique sur les formes de la poésie lyrique en France depuis la Renaissance.* 2nd ed. Paris, 1912. 615 pp.

Organized by form; summaries in appendix.

1111 Mölk, Ulrich, and Frederick Wolfzettel. *Répertoire métrique de la poésie française des origines à 1350.* Munich: Wilhelm Fink, 1972. 682 pp.

Including indexing and referencing by color-coded punched cards in a slipcase.

1112 Pfrommer, Walter. *Grundzüge der Strophenentwicklung in der französische Lyrik von Baudelaire zu Apollinaire.* Diss., Tübingen, 1963. 185 pp.

STUDIES

1113 Abraham, Claude K. *Enfin Malherbe: The Influence of Malherbe on French Lyric Prosody, 1605-1674.* Lexington: University Press of Kentucky, 1971. 384 pp.

VERSE SYSTEMS

1114 Baehr, Rudolf. "Rhythm and Rhyme in French Poetry from Baudelaire to Aragon." *Sprachkunst* 12 (1981): 348–63.

1115 Berghe, Christian L. van den. *La Phonostylistique du français*. The Hague: Mouton, 1976. 556 pp.

❖ Burger, Michel [720].

1116 Chambers, Frank M. *An Introduction to Old Provençal Versification*. Philadelphia: American Philosophical Society, 1985. 299 pp.

1117 Chatelain, Henri. *Recherches sur le vers français au XVe siècle: Rimes, mètres, et strophes*. Paris: Champion, 1908. 269 pp.

1118 Claudel, Paul. "Réflexions et propositions sur le vers français." *Réflexions sur la poésie*. Paris: Gallimard, 1963, 1966. Pp. 7–90.

1119 Cohen, Jean. *Structure du langage poétique*. Paris: Flammarion, 1966. 231 pp.

❖ Cornulier, Benoît de [107].

1120 ———. *Théorie du vers: Rimbaud, Verlaine, Mallarmé*. Paris: du Seuil, 1982. 320 pp.

1121 ———. "Versifier: Le Code et sa règle." *Poétique*, no. 66 (1986): 191–97.

1122 Delbouille, Paul. *Poésie et sonorités: La Critique contemporaine devant le pouvoir suggestif des sons*. 2 vols. Paris: Société d'Édition "Les Belles Lettres," 1961, 1984.

1123 Dragonetti, Roger. *La Technique poétique des trouvères dans la chanson courtoise*. Bruges: De Tempel, 1960. 702 pp.

1124 Elwert, W. Theodor. *Französische Metrik*. 4th ed. Munich: Hueber, 1978. 204 pp.

1125 Flescher, Jacqueline. "French [Versification]." In Wimsatt, ed. [60], pp. 177–90.

1126 Fotitch, Tatiana. "Romance Prosody." *Princeton Encyclopedia* [55], pp. 713–15.

1127 Grammont, Maurice. *Petit traité de la versification français*. Paris, 1908; 10th ed. 1982.

1128 Guiette, Robert. *D'une poésie formelle en France au Moyen Age*. Ghent: University of Ghent, 1960.

1129 Guiraud, Pierre. *Essais de stylistique*. Paris: Klincksieck, 1969.

1130 ———. "Les Fonctions sécondaires du langage." *Le Langage*. Vol. 25 of *Encyclopédie de la Pleiade*. Paris: Gallimard, 1968. Pp. 435–512.

1131 ———. *Langage et versification d'après l'oeuvre de Paul Valéry*. Paris: Klincksieck, 1953.

1132 ———. *La Versification*. 2nd ed. Paris: Presses Universitaires de France, 1973. 128 pp.

1133 Hatcher, Anne G., and Mark Musa. "Rhyme Schemes in Provençal Poetry." *Romance Philology* 38 (1984): 171–99.

1134 Hillery, David. *Music and Poetry in France from Baudelaire to Mallarmé: An Essay on Poetic Theory and Practice*. Bern: Peter Lang, 1980. 154 pp.

1135 Humiston, C. C. *A Comparative Study of the Metrical Technique of Ronsard and Malherbe*. University of California Publications in Modern Philology, vol. 24, no. 1. Berkeley and Los Angeles: University of California Press, 1941. Pp. 1–180.

1136 Hyatte, Reginald. "Meter and Rhythm in Jean Antoine de Baïf's *Entrénes de poézie fransoeze* and the *Vers mesurés à l'antique* of Other Poets in the Late Sixteenth Century." *Bibliothèque d'Humanisme et Renaissance* 43 (1981): 488–508.

1137 Ince, Walter. "Some of Valéry's Reflections on Rhythm." *Baudelaire, Mallarmé, Valéry: New Essays in Honour of Lloyd Austin*. Ed. Malcolm Bowie et al. Cambridge: Cambridge University Press, 1982. Pp. 384–97.

❖ Jeanroy, Alfred [503].

❖ Jones, P. Mansell [540].

1138 Kastner, L. E. "Histoire des termes techniques de la versification française." *Revue des Langues Romanes* 47 (1904): 5–28.

1139 Kibédi Varga, A. *Les Constantes du poème: Analyse du langage poétique*. Paris: Picard, 1977. 298 pp.

1140 Körting, Gustav. "Rhythmik." *Encyclopaedie und Methodologie der romanische Philologie*. 3 vols. Heilbronn, 1884–88. Vol. 2, pp. 408–40.

1141 Kristeva, Julia. "Contraintes rythmiques et langage poétique." *Polylogue*. Paris: du Seuil, 1977. Pp. 437–66.

1142 Lausberg, Heinrich. "Zur altfranzösischen Metrik." *Archiv* 191 (1955): 183–217.

❖ Leakey, F. W. [164].

1143 Lechantre, Michel. "P(h)o(n)étique." *Poétique et poésie*. Vol. 1 of the *Cahiers Paul Valéry*. Ed. Jean Levaillant. 3 vols. Paris: Gallimard, 1975. Pp. 91–122.

1144 Lewis, Roy. *On Reading French Verse: A Study of Poetic Form*. Oxford: Clarendon Press, 1982. 256 pp.

❖ Maillard, Jean [363].

1145 Martinon, Philippe. *Dictionnaire des rimes françaises, précédé d'un traité de versification*. 2nd ed., rev. by R. Lacroix de L'Isle. Paris: Larousse, 1971.

1146 Mazaleyrat, Jean. *Éléments de métrique française*. 3rd ed. Paris: Armand-Colin, 1981. 232 pp.

1147 ———. "Le Mètre," "Le Rythme," "Le Vers." *Grand Larousse de la langue française*. Paris: Larousse, 1971–78. Vol. 4, pp. 3347–52; vol. 6, pp. 5302–10; vol. 7, pp. 6436–44.

❖   ———. [1100].

❖   Meschonnic, Henri [228].

1148 ———, ed. *Poétique du vers francais*. Paris, 1974.

1149 Meyer, Paul. "Le Couplet de deux vers." *Romania* 23 (1894): 1–35.

1150 Mölk, Ulrich. "Troubadour Versification as Literary Craftsmanship." *L'Esprit créateur* 19, no. 4 (1979): 3–16.

1151 ———. "Zur Metrik der Trobadors." In *GRLM* [1103], vol. 2, *Les Genres lyriques*, part 1, no. 3, 1987. Pp. 29–44.

1152 Mohr, Wolfgang. "Romanische Versmasse und Strophenformen (im Deutschen)." *Reallexikon II* [1182], vol. 3, pp. 557–78.

❖   Morier, Henri [549].

1153 Parent, Monique, ed. *Le Vers français au 20e siècle*. Paris: Klincksieck, 1967. 323 pp.

       Includes sixteen papers and discussions on theory and practice.

1154 Pineau, Joseph. *Le Mouvement rythmique en francais: Principes et méthode d'analyse*. Paris: Klincksieck, 1979. 215 pp.

1155 "Provençal Versification." *North British Review* 53 (1871): 317–50.

1156 Quicherat, Louis M. *Petit traité de versification française*. 15th ed. Paris, 1915. 137 pp.

1157 ———. *Traité de versification française*. 2nd ed. Paris, 1850. 587 pp.

1158 Roubaud, Jacques. *La Vieillesse d'Alexandre: Essai sur quelques états récents du vers francais*. Paris: Maspero, 1978. 215 pp.

1159 Ruwet, Nicolas. *Langage, musique, poésie*. Paris: du Seuil, 1972. 247 pp.

1160 ———. "Linguistique et poétique: Une brève introduction." *Français Moderne* 49 (1981): 1–19.

1161 Scarfe, Francis. *The Art of Paul Valéry*. London: Heinemann, 1954.

1162 Scott, Clive. *French Verse-Art: A Study*. Cambridge: Cambridge University Press, 1980. 252 pp.

1163 ———. *A Question of Syllables: Essays in Nineteenth-Century French Verse*. Cambridge: Cambridge University Press, 1986. 215 pp.

❖ Seaman, David W. [581].

1164 Smith, Nathaniel B. *Figures of Repetition in the Old Provençal Lyric: A Study of the Style of the Troubadours.* Chapel Hill: University of North Carolina Press, 1976. 317 pp.

1165 Spire, André. *Plaisir poétique et plaisir musculaire: Essai sur l'évolution des techniques poétiques.* Paris: S. F. Vanni, 1949. 547 pp.

1166 Stengel, Edmund. "Lehre von der romanische Sprachkunst: Romanische Verslehre." In Gröber's *Grundriss* [1102], vol. 2, part 1, pp. 1–90.

1167 Stimpson, Brian. *Paul Valéry and Music: A Study of the Techniques of Composition in Valéry's Poetry.* Cambridge: Cambridge University Press, 1984. 339 pp.

1168 Thomas, L.-P. *Le Vers moderne: Ses moyens d'expression, son esthétique.* Brussels: Palais des Académics, 1943.

1169 Tobler, Adolf. *Vom altfranzösischen Versbau alter und neuer Zeit.* 5th ed. Leipzig, 1910. 177 pp.

1170 Träger, Ernst. *Geschichte des Alexandriners.* Part 1: *Der französische Alexandriner bis Ronsard.* Leipzig, 1889. Part 2 never published.

1171 Valéry, Paul. *The Art of Poetry.* Trans. Denise Folliot. Vol. 7 of *The Collected Works of Paul Valéry.* New York: Pantheon, 1958. 345 pp.

1172 Volkoff, Vladimir. *Vers une métrique française.* Columbia, S.C.: French Literature Publications, 1978. 200 pp.

1173 Werf, Hendrik van der. *The Chansons of the Troubadours and Trouvères: A Study of the Melodies and Their Relation to the Poems.* Utrecht: A. Dosthoek, 1972. 166 pp.

1174 Zumthor, Paul. *Essai de poétique médiévale.* Paris: du Seuil, 1972. 518 pp.

GERMAN AND SCANDINAVIAN

BIBLIOGRAPHIES

1175 *Germanistik.* 1960– (quarterly).

Current bibliography; occasional paragraph reviews.

1176 Hollander, Lee M. "General Commentaries on Skaldic Verse: Metrics, Style, Origins, Etc." *A Bibliography of Skaldic Studies.* Copenhagen: Ejnar Munksgaard, 1958. Pp. 27–55.

1177 *Jahresberichte über die Erscheinungen auf dem Gebiete der germanische Philologie.* Vols. 1–42; n.s. vols. 1–19. Berlin, 1879–1939.

Thorough coverage of works published in German territories.

1178 *Jahresberichte für neuere deutsche Literaturgeschichte*, n.s., vols. 1–19. Stuttgart, 1890–1919.

S.v. "Metrik."

1179 Kossmann, Bernard, ed. *Bibliographie der deutsche Sprach- und Literaturwissenschaft.* 1960–.

S.v. "Literaturwissenschaft: Metrik."

ENCYCLOPEDIAS, DICTIONARIES

1180 Paul, Hermann, ed. *Grundriss der germanischen Philologie.* 2nd ed. Strassburg: Trübner, 1905. Vol. 2, pt. 2.

Four long review essays on Old High German, Middle High German, Old English, and Middle English.

1181 *Reallexikon der deutschen Literaturgeschichte.* Ed. Paul Merker and Wolfgang Stammler. 1st ed. 4 vols. Berlin, 1925–31.

Still very much worth consulting, for the first edition cites numerous short entries on specific terms, forms, and meters which are only covered in longer survey entries in the second edition [1182].

1182 *Reallexikon der deutschen Literaturgeschichte.* Ed. Werner Kohlschmidt and Wolfgang Mohr (vols. 1–3), Klaus Kanzog and Achem Masser (vol. 4). 2nd ed. 4 vols. Berlin: De Gruyter, 1958–84.

1183 Stammler, Wolfgang, ed. *Deutsche Philologie im Aufriss.* 2nd. ed. 3 vols. Berlin: E. Schmidt, 1957–62.

HISTORIES

1184 Atkins, Henry G. *A History of German Versification: Ten Centuries of Metrical Evolution.* London: Methuen, 1923. 276 pp.

1185 Heusler, Andreas. *Deutsche Versgeschichte, mit Einschluss des altenglischen und altnordischen Stabreimverses.* 3 vols. Berlin: De Gruyter, 1925–29; rpt. (as 2nd ed.) 1956.

1186 Lehmann, Winfred P. *The Development of Germanic Verse Form.* Austin: University of Texas Press, 1956. 217 pp.

1187 Pretzel, Ulrich, with supp. by Helmuth Thomas. "Deutsche Verskunst." In Stammler [1183], cols. 2357–2546; rpt. in Pretzel's *Kleine Schriften.* Ed. Wolfgang Bachofer et al. Berlin: E. Schmidt, 1979. Pp. 295–372.

Stanza Indexes

1188   Frank, Horst J. *Handbuch der deutschen Strophenformen*. Munich: Hanser, 1980. 885 pp.

1189   Schlawe, Fritz. *Die deutsche Strophenformen: Systematisch- chronologische Register zur deutschen Lyrik 1600–1950*. Stuttgart: Metzler, 1972. 578 pp.

1190   Touber, A. H. *Deutsche Strophenformen des Mittelalters*. Stuttgart: Metzler, 1975. 164 pp.

Studies

1191   Baesecke, Georg. *Kleine Metrische Schriften*. Ed. Werner Schröder. Munich: Wilhelm Fink, 1968. 218 pp.

1192   Bausinger, Hermann. *Formen der "Volkspoesie."* 2nd ed., rev. Berlin: Schmidt, 1980. 312 pp.

1193   Belmore, H. W. *Rilke's Craftsmanship: An Analysis of His Poetic Style*. Oxford: Basil Blackwell, 1954. 234 pp.

1194   Beyschlag, Siegfried. *Altdeutsche Verskunst in Grundzügen*. 6th ed. Nürnberg. H. Carl, 1969.

1195   Binder, Wolfgang. "Hölderlins Verskunst." *Hölderlin-Jahrbuch* 23 (1982–83): 10–33.

 ❖   Birkenhauer, Renate [103].

1196   Bostock, J. Knight. "Appendix on Old Saxon and Old High German Metre." *Handbook of Old High German Literature*. 2nd ed. Oxford: Clarendon Press, 1976. Pp. 302–26.

1197   Breuer, Dieter. *Deutsche Metrik und Versgeschichte*. Munich: Wilhelm Fink, 1981. 414 pp.

1198   Brody, Elaine, and R. A. Fowkes. *The German Lied and Its Poetry*. New York: New York University Press, 1971. 316 pp.

1199   Chisholm, David. *Goethe's Knittelvers: A Prosodic Analysis*. Bonn: Bouvier, 1975. 213 pp.

1200   ———. "Phonological Aspects of German Verse and Literary Prose." *Siegener Periodicum zur internat. empirischen Literaturwissenschaft* 3 (1984): 119–40.

1201   ———. "Phonological Patterning in English and German Verse: A Computer-assisted Approach." *Quantitative Linguistics* 14 (1982): 114–46.

1202   ———. "Phonological Patterning in German Verse." *Computers and the Humanities* 10 (1976): 5–20.

1203   Chisholm, David, and Steven Sondrup. *Konkordanz zu den Gedichten Conrad Ferdinand Meyers. Mit einem Versmass- und Reimschemaindex*. Tübingen: Max Niemeyer, 1982. 601 pp.

1204 Closs, August. *Die freien Rhythmen in der deutschen Lyrik*. Bern: A. Francke, 1947. 198 pp.

1205 De Boor, Helmut. *Kleine Schriften*. Ed. R. Wisniewski and H. Kolb. 2 vols. Berlin: De Gruyter, 1966. Vol. 2.

1206 Ernst, Ulrich. *Der Liber Evangeliorum Otfrids von Weissenburg: Literarästhetik und Verstechnik in Licht der Tradition*. Cologne and Vienna: Böhlau, 1975.

❖ Ernst, Ulrich, and Peter Erich Neuser, eds. [112].

1207 Frank, Roberta. *Old Norse Court Poetry: The Dróttkvaett Stanza*. Ithaca: Cornell University Press, 1978.

❖ Grimm, Wilhelm Karl [148].

❖ Habermann, Paul, and Klaus Kanzog [21].

1208 Hallberg, Peter. *Old Icelandic Poetry: Eddic Lay and Skaldic Verse*. Lincoln: University of Nebraska Press, 1975. 219 pp.

1209 Hellmuth, Hans-Heinrich. *Metrische Erfindung und metrische Theorie bei Klopstock*. Munich: Wilhelm Fink, 1973. 212 pp.

1210 Hinderschiedt, Ingeborg. *Zur Heliandmetrik: Das Verhältnis von Rhythmus und Satzgewicht im Altsächsischen*. Amsterdam: John Benjamins, 1979. 143 pp.

1211 Hoffmann, Werner. *Altdeutsche Metrik*. Stuttgart: Metzler, 1967.

1212 Hollander, Lee M. Introduction. *The Skalds*. Princeton: Princeton University Press, 1945; rpt. Ann Arbor: University of Michigan Press, 1968. Pp. 1–24.

1213 Hügli, Emil. *Die romanischen Strophen in der Dichtung deutscher Romantiker*. Zurich, 1900. 102 pp.

1214 Jellinek, M. H. "Studien zu den älteren deutschen Grammatikern: Die Lehre von Akzent und Quantität." *Zeitschrift für deutsches Altertum und deutsche Literatur* 48 (1906): 227–363.

1215 Jost, Walter. *Probleme und Theorien der deutschen und englischen Verslehre*. Bern: Herbert Lang, 1976. 275 pp.

1216 Kabell, Aage. *Metrische Studien I: Der Alliterationsvers*. Munich: Wilhelm Fink, 1978. 313 pp.

1217 ———. *Studier i Metrik, III: Systematisk*. Copenhagen: Rosenkilde & Bagger, 1952. 200 pp.

1218 Kauffmann, Friedrich. *Deutsche Metrik nach ihrer geschichtlichen Entwicklung*. 3rd ed. Marburg, 1912.

1219 Kayser, Wolfgang. *Das sprachliche Kunstwerk*. 15th ed. Munich: A. Francke, 1971.

1220 Kieffer, Bruce. "Goethe's Metrics and His Classical Elegies." *DAI* 40, 3A (1979): 1492 (Princeton). 197 pp.

1221 Köneke, Bruno. *Untersuchungen zum frühmittelhochdeutschen Versbau.* Munich: Wilhelm Fink, 1976. 316 pp.

1222 Kreutzer, Gert. *Die Dichtungslehre der Skalden: Poetologische Terminologie und Autorenkommentare als Grundlagen für eine Gattungspoetik der Skaldendichtung.* 2nd ed., rev. Mesienheim am Glan: Hain, 1977. 313 pp.

1223 Kühnel, J. B. *Untersuchungen zum germanischen Stabreimvers.* Göppingen: Kümmerle, 1978. 397 pp.

1224 Kuhn, Hans. *Sprachgeschichte. Verskunst.* Vol. 1 of his *Kleine Schriften.* Berlin: De Gruyter, 1969. 527 pp.

1225 ———. "Westgermanisches in der altnordischen Verskunst." *Beiträge zur Geschichte der deutsche Sprache und Literatur* 63 (1939): 178–236.

1226 ———. "Wortstellung und -betonung im Altgermanischen." *Beiträge zur Geschichte der deutsche Sprache und Literatur* 57 (1933): 1–109.

1227 Kuhn, Hugo. *Minnesanges Wende.* 2nd ed. Tübingen: Max Niemeyer, 1967.

1228 Lachmann, Karl. "Über althochdeutsche Betonung und Verskunst." Rpt. in his *Kleinere Schriften.* Ed. Karl Müllenhoff. Berlin, 1876. Pp. 358–406.

1229 Lehmann, Winfred P. "Germanic [Versification]." In Wimsatt, ed. [60], pp. 122–35.

1230 McLintock, D. R. "Metre and Rhythm in the *Hildebrandslied.*" *Modern Language Review* 71 (1976): 565–76.

1231 Magnuson, Karl. "Phonological Investigations into the Structure of German Verse." Diss., University of Michigan, 1966.

1232 Marstrander, Carl. "Notes on Alliteration." *Serta Eitremiana: Opuscula Philologica S. Eitrem.* Oslo: A. W. Brøgger, 1942. Pp. 185–208.

1233 Meyer, Hans G. *Die Strophenfolge und ihre Gesetzmassigkeiten im Minnelied Walthers von der Vogelweide: Ein Beitrag zur inneren Form hochmittelalterlicher Lyrik.* Königstein: Hain, 1981. 574 pp.

1234 Meyer, Hermann. "Von Leben der Strophe in neuerer deutscher Lyrik." *Deutsche Vierteljahrsschrift* 25 (1951): 436–73.

1235 Minor, Jakob. *Neuhochdeutsche Metrik.* 2nd ed. Strassburg, 1902. 537 pp.

❖ Mohr, Wolfgang [229].

1236 Nagel, Bert. *Der deutsche Meistersang: Poetische Technik, musikalische Form und Sprachgestaltung der Meistersinger.* Heidelberg: F. H. Kerle, 1952.

❖ ———. [123].

1237 Neumann, Friedrich. "Deutsche Literatur bis 1500: Versgeschichte (Metrik)." *Kurzer Grundriss der germanischen Philologie.* Ed. L. E. Schmitt. 2 vols. Berlin: De Gruyter, 1971. Vol. 2, pp. 608–65.

1238 ———. *Geschichte des neuhochdeutschen Reimes von Opitz bis Wieland*. Berlin, 1920.

1239 Newton, Robert P. *Form in the "Menschheitsdämmerung": A Study of Prosodic Elements and Style in German Expressionist Poetry*. The Hague: Mouton, 1971. 270 pp.

❖ ———. *Vowel Undersong* [79].

1240 Paetzel, Walther. *Die Variationen in der altgermanischen Alliterationspoesie*. Berlin, 1913. 216 pp.

1241 Patzlaff, Rainer. *Otfrid von Weissenburg und die mittelalterliche "versus"-Tradition: Untersuchungen zur Formgeschichtlichen Stellung der Otfridstrophe*. Tübingen: Max Niemeyer, 1975. 254 pp.

1242 Paul, Hermann. "Deutsche Metrik." In Paul, ed. [1180], pp. 39–140.

1243 Paul, Otto, and Ingeborg Glier. *Deutsche Metrik*. 9th ed. Munich: M. Hueber, 1974.

1244 Pohl, Gerhard. *Der Strophenbau im deutschen Volkslied*. Palaestra, no. 136. Berlin, 1921. 219 pp.

❖ Pretzel, Ulrich [130].

❖ Ranawake, Silvia [510].

1245 Saran, Fritz. "Metrik." *Ergebnisse und Fortschritte der germanischen Wissenschaft im letzten Vierteljahrhundert*. Ed. Richard Bethge. Leipzig, 1902. Pp. 158–87.

❖ Sayce, Olive [512].

1246 ———, ed. *Poets of the Minnesang*. Oxford: Clarendon Press, 1967.

1247 Schädle, Lucie. *Der frühe deutsche Blankvers unter besonderer Berücksichtigung seiner Verwendung durch Chr. M. Wieland*. Göttingen: A. Kummerle, 1972. 272 pp.

1248 Schödlbauer, Ulrich. "Odenform und freier Vers: Antike Formmotiv in moderner Dichtung." *Literaturwissenschaftliches Jahrbuch* 23 (1982): 191–206.

1249 Schultz, Hartwig. *Form als Inhalt: Vers- und Sinnstrukturen bei Joseph von Eichendorff, Annette von Droste-Hulshoff*. Bonn: Bouvier, 1981. 438 pp.

❖ Seckel, Dietrich [201].

1250 See, Klaus von. *Skaldendichtung: Eine Einführung*. Munich: Artemis, 1980. 108 pp.

1251 Sievers, Eduard. *Altgermanische Metrik*. Halle, 1893.

1252 ———. *Rhythmisch-melodische Studien: Vorträge und Aufsätze.* Heidelberg: Carl Winter, 1912. 141 pp.

1253 Storz, Gerhard. *Der Vers in der neueren deutschen Dichtung.* Stuttgart: Reclam, 1970. 239 pp.

❖ Suppan, Wolfgang [331].

1254 Taylor, Ronald J. *The Art of the Minnesanger: Songs of the Thirteenth Century Transcribed and Edited with Commentaries.* 2 vols. Cardiff: University of Wales Press, 1968. Vol. 2.

1255 Thieme, Klaus Dieter. *Zum Problem des rhythmischen Satzschlusses in der deutschen Literatur des Spätmittelalters.* Munich: Max Hueber, 1965. 171 pp.

1256 Wagenknecht, Christian. *Deutsche Metrik: Eine historische Einführung.* Munich: C. H. Beck, 1981. 139 pp.

1257 Walshe, M. O. "A Metrical Survey." *Medieval German Literature: A Survey.* Cambridge, Mass.: Harvard University Press, 1962. Pp. 71–85.

1258 Wetzel, Heinz. *Klang und Bild in der Dichtung Georg Trakls.* Göttingen: Vandenhoeck & Ruprecht, 1968.

❖ Wolf, Ferdinand [367].

1259 *Zu Form und Bau mittelalterlicher Dichtung.* Ed. Friedrich Maurer. Special Issue of *Der Deutschunterricht* 11, no. 2 (1959).

Six essays and a bibliography.

SPANISH

BIBLIOGRAPHIES

1260 Carballo Picazo, Alfredo. *Métrica española.* Madrid: Instituto de Estudios Madrileños, 1956. 161 pp.

Lists 1203 works, fifteenth through twentieth centuries. Divided into General Studies (subdivided by century, then alphabetically), then Specialized Studies (alphabetical only). Index. Numbered entries.

1261 Clarke, Dorothy Clotelle. *Una Bibliografia de versificación española.* University of California Publications in Modern Philology, vol. 20, no. 2. Berkeley and Los Angeles: University of California Press, 1937. Pp. 57–126.

A single alphabetical, unnumbered listing with subject index.

1262 *Revista de filologia española.* 1918–.

Annual bibliography of current research.

STANZA INDEXES

1263 Tavani, Giuseppe. *Repertorio metrico della lirica galego-portoghese*. Rome: Edizioni dell'Ateneo, 1967.

STUDIES

1264 Adams, Kenneth. "Further Aspects of Sound-Patterning in the *Poema de Mio Cid*." *Hispanic Review* 48 (1980): 449–67.

1265 Alonso, Dámaso. *Poesía española: Ensayo de metodos y limites estilisticos*. Madrid: Editorial Gredos, 1950.

1266 Baehr, Rudolf. *Spanische Verslehre auf historischer Grundlage*. Tübingen: Max Niemeyer, 1962; 2nd ed., rev., 1970; trans. K. Wagner and F. López Estrada as *Manual de versificación española*. 325 pp.

❖ Bec, Pierre [489].

1267 Benot y Rodriguez, Eduardo. *Prosodia castellana i versificación*. 3 vols. Madrid, 1892.

❖ Burger, Michel [720].

1268 Clarke, Dorothy Clotelle. *A Chronological Sketch of Castilian Versification Together with a List of Its Metric Terms*. University of California Publications in Modern Philology, vol. 34, no. 3. Berkeley and Los Angeles: University of California Press, 1932. Pp. 279–381.

❖ ———. "The Early Seguidilla" [419].

1269 ———. "The Early Spanish Octosyllable: Galician-Portuguese and Provençal Origins." *Hispanic Review* 10 (1942): 1–11.

1270 ———. *Morphology of Fifteenth-Century Castilian Verse*. Pittsburgh: Duquesne University Press, 1964. 233 pp.

1271 ———. "Nebrija on Versification." *PMLA* 72 (1957): 27–42.

1272 Cunha, Celso F., da. *Estudos de versificaçao portuguesa (seculos XIII a XVI)*. Paris: Fundaçao Calouste Gulbenkian, Centro Cultural Portugues, 1982.

1273 Davison, Ned J. *Sound Patterns in a Poem of José Martí: An Examination of Phonemic Structures and Poetic Musicality*. Salt Lake City: Damuir Press, 1975. 118 pp.

1274 Diez, Friedrich. "Form." *Über die erste portugiesische Kunst- und Hofpoesie*. Bonn, 1863. Pp. 36–72.

1275 Díez de Revenga, Francisco J. *La métrica de los poetas del 27*. Murcia: Universidad Departmento de Literatura Español, 1973. 434 pp.

1276 Díez Echarri, Emiliano. *Teorías métricas del siglo de oro*. Madrid: Consejo Superior de Investigaciones Científices, Instituto "Miguel de Cervantes," 1949; rpt. 1971. 355 pp.

1277 Dodd, Steven. "An Algorithm for Determining the Metre of Spanish Verse." *Bulletin of the Association for Literary and Linguistic Computing* 8 (1980): 20–27.

1278 Domínguez Capparós, José. *Contribución a la historia de las teorías métricas en los siglos XVIII y XIX*. Madrid: Impr. Aguirre, 1975. 544 pp.

1279 Faulhaber, Charles B. "Medieval Spanish Metrical Terminology and MS. 9589 of the Biblioteca Nacional, Madrid." *Romance Philology* 33 (1979): 43–61.

1280 Foster, David W. "Appendix on Ballad Metrics." *The Early Spanish Ballad*. New York: Twayne, 1981. Pp. 184–88.

1281 Hall, R. A., Jr. "Old Spanish Stress-Timed Verse and the German Superstratum." *Romance Philology* 19 (1965): 227–34.

1282 Henriquez Ureña, Pedro. *Estudios de versificación española*. Buenos Aires: Universidad de Buenos Aires Departmento Editorial, 1961.

1283 Kloe, Donald R. *A Dictionary of Onomatopoeic Sounds, Tones, and Noises in English and Spanish*. Detroit, 1977. 153 pp.

1284 Le Gentil, Pierre. "Discussions sur la versification espagnole médiévale: à propos d'un livre récent." *Romance Philology* 12 (1958): 1–32.

1285 ———. *La Poésie lyrique espagnole et portugaise à la fin du Moyen Age*. 2 vols. Rennes, 1949–53. Vol. 2, *Les Formes*. 505 pp.

1286 López Estrada, Francisco. *Métrica española del siglo XX*. Madrid: Editorial Gredos, 1974. 226 pp.

1287 Meyer, Paul. "Traités catalans de grammaire et de poétique." *Romania* 6 (1877): 341–58.

1288 Morley, S. Griswold. "Recent Theories about the Meter of the Cid." *PMLA* 48 (1933): 965–80.

1289 ———. *Studies in Spanish Dramatic Versification of the Siglo de Oro*. University of California Publications in Modern Philology, vol. 7, no. 3. Berkeley and Los Angeles: University of California Press, 1918. Pp. 131–73.

1290 Navarro Tomás, Tomás. *Métrica española: Reseña histórica y descriptiva*. Syracuse: Syracuse University Press, 1956. 556 pp.

1291 Nelson, Lowry, Jr. "Spanish [Versification]." In Wimsatt, ed. [60], pp. 165–76.

1292 Oliva, Salvador. *Métrica catalana*. Barcelona: Quaderns Crema, 1980.

1293 Piera, Carlos José. "Spanish Verse and the Theory of Meter." *DAI* 42, 1A (1981): 197 (UCLA.). 251 pp.

1294 Quilis, Antonio. *Métrica española*. 3rd ed., rev. and enl. Barcelona: Editorial Ariel, 1986. 211 pp.

1295 Smith, Colin. "Metrical Structures." *The Making of the "Poema de mio Cid."* Cambridge: Cambridge University Press, 1983. Pp. 104–36.

1296 Spang, Kurt. *Ritmo y versificación: Teoría y práctica del análysis métrico y rítmico.* Murcia: Universidad de Murcia, 1983. 221 pp.

❖ Stern, Samuel M. [1444].

1297 Tavani, Giuseppe. "Considerazioni sulle origini dell' 'arte mayor.'" *Cultura Neolatina* 25 (1965): 15–33.

❖ Webber, Ruth D. [321].

ITALIAN

ENCYCLOPEDIAS, DICTIONARIES

1298 Mari, Giovanni. *Riassunto e dizionarietto di ritmica italiana con saggi dell'uso dantesco e petrarchesco.* Turin, 1901.

1299 Memmo, Francesco Paolo. *Dizionario di metrica italiana.* Rome: Edizioni dell'Ateneo, 1983. 182 pp.

STANZA INDEXES

1300 Solimena, Adriana. *Repertorio metrico dello Stil novo.* Rome: Società Filologica Romana, 1980. 235 pp.

STUDIES

1301 Avalle, D'Arco Silvio. *Preistoria dell'endecasillabo.* Milan: R. Ricardi, 1963.

1302 Baldelli, Ignazio. "Endecasillabo," "Rima," "Sestina, S. Doppia," "Terzina." *Enciclopedia dantesca.* Ed. Giorgio Petrocchi et al. 5 vols. + Supp. Florence: Istituto dell'Enciclopedia Italiana, 1970–78. Vol. 2, pp. 672–76; vol. 4, pp. 930–49; vol. 5, pp. 193–95, 583–94.

1303 Barber, Joseph A. "Petrarch's Use of the Metric Figures in the *Canzoniere*." *Modern Language Notes* 95 (1980): 1–38.

1304 ———. "Rhyme Scheme Patterns in Petrarch's *Canzoniere*." *Modern Language Notes* 92 (1977): 139–46.

1305 Beccaria, Gian Luigi. *L'Autonomia del significante: Figure del ritmo e della sintassi Dante, Pascoli, D'Annunzio.* Turin: Giulio Einaudi, 1975. 357 pp.

1306 ———. "Ritmo." *Enciclopedia dantesca* [1302], vol. 4, pp. 985–92.

1307 Beltrami, Pietro G. *Metrica, poetica, metrica dantesca.* Pisa: Pacini, 1981. 163 pp.

1308 ———. "Prospettive della metrica." *Lingua e stile* 15 (1980): 281–300. English summary, p. 303.

❖ Bertinetto, P. M. [204].

1309 ———. *Strutture prosodiche dell'italiano. Accento, quantità, sillaba, giuntura, fondamenti metrici.* Florence: Presso l'Academia della Crusca, 1981. 317 pp.

❖ Biadene, Leandro [430].

1310 Boyde, Patrick. "A Note on Dante's Metric and Versification." *Dante's Lyric Poetry.* Ed. K. Foster and Patrick Boyde. 2 vols. Oxford: Clarendon Press, 1967. Vol. 1, pp. xliv–lv.

1311 ———. "The Hendecasyllable." *Dante's Style in His Lyric Poetry.* 2nd ed. Cambridge: Cambridge University Press, 1971. Pp. 209–36.

❖ Burger, Michel [720].

1312 Carducci, Giosue, ed. *La poesia barbara nei secoli XV e XVI.* Bologna, 1881.

1313 Chiarini, Giuseppe. "I critici italiani e la metrica delle *Odi barbare.*" Preface to Carducci's *Odi barbare.* 2nd ed. Bologna, 1878.

1314 ———. "La nuova metrica della poesia italiana." *Nuova antologia,* 2nd ser. 8 (1878): 463–96.

❖ Cremante, Renzo, and Mario Pazzaglia, eds. [11], part 2 on Italian.

1315 Dionisotti, C. "Ragioni metriche del Quattrocento." *Giornale storico della letteratura italiana* 124 (1947): 1–34.

1316 Elwert, W. Theodor. *Italienische Metrik.* 2nd ed., rev. Wiesbaden: Franz Steiner, 1984. 196 pp.

1317 Flamini, Francesco. *Notizia storica dei versi i metri italiani dal medioevo ai tempi nostri.* Livorno, 1918. 140 pp.

❖ Freccero, John [471].

1318 Fubini, Mario. *Metrica e poesia: Lezioni sulle forme metriche italiane.* 2nd ed., rev. Milan: Feltrinelli, 1970.

1319 Giamatti, A. Bartlett. "Italian [Versification]." In Wimsatt, ed. [60], pp. 148–64.

1320 Grandgent, C. H. "Dante's Verse." *Studies in Philology* 17 (1920): 1–18.

1321 Haller, Robert S., ed. and trans. *Literary Criticism of Dante Alighieri.* Lincoln: University of Nebraska Press, 1973. 192 pp.

❖ Ker, W. P. "De Superbia Carminum." In Ker [29], pp. 332–37.

1322 Leonetti, Pasquale. *Storia della tecnica del verso italiano.* 2 parts in 3 vols. Naples, 1934–38.

1323 Levi, Attilio. "Della versificazione italiana." *Archivum Romanicum* 14 (1930): 449–506.

❖ Limentani, Alberto [388].

1324 Macri, Oreste. *Semantica e metrica dei "Sepolcri" del Fascolo, con una teoria dell'endecasillabo.* Rome: Bulzoni, 1978. 409 pp.

1325 D'Ovidio, Francesco. "Sull'origine dei versi italiana." *Versificazione italiana e arte poetica medievale.* Milan, 1910; rpt. in Cremante and Pazzaglia, eds. [11].

1326 ———. *Versificazione romanza: Poetica e poesia medievale.* 3 vols. Naples: A. Guida, 1932.

1327 Pazzaglia, Mario. *Teoria e analisi metrica.* Bologna: Patron, 1974. 268 pp.

1328 ———. *Il verso e l'arte della Canzone nel De vulgari Eloquentia.* Florence: La Nuova Italia, 1967. 214 pp.

1329 Pernicone, Vincenzo. "Storia e svolgimento della metrica." *Tecnica e teoria letteraria.* Ed. A. Momigliano. 2nd ed. Milan: C. Marzorati, 1951. Pp. 297–349.

1330 Pirotti, Umberto. *L'endecasillabo dattilico e altri studi di letteratura italiana.* Bologna: Patron, 1979. 201 pp.

❖ Riesz, János [428].

1331 Sansone, Giuseppe E. "Per un'analisi strutturale dell'endecasillabo." *Lingua e stile* 2 (1967): 179–97.

1332 Scaglione, Aldo D. "Periodic Syntax and Flexible Meter in the *Divina Commedia.*" *Romance Philology* 21 (1967): 1–22.

1333 Serretta, M. *Endecasillabi crescenti nella poesia italiana delle origini nel canzoniere del Petrarca.* Milan: Società editrice "Vita e pensiero," 1938. 245 pp.

1334 Sesini, U. "L'endecasillabo: struttura e peculiarita." *Convivium* 11 (1939): 545–70.

1335 Steadman, John M. "Verse without Rime: Sixteenth-Century Italian Defences of Versi Sciolti." *Italica* 41 (1964): 384–402.

1336 Tempo, Antonio da. *Summa artis ritmici vulgaris dictaminis* (1332). Ed. Richard Andrews. Bologna: Commissione per i testi di lingua, 1977. 143 pp.

❖ Thomas, Walter [732], chap. 3.

❖ Wilkins, Ernest Hatch [456].

1337 Wlassics, Tibor. *Interpretazione di prosodia dantesca.* Rome: Signorelli, 1972. 161 pp.

SLAVIC

BIBLIOGRAPHIES

1338 Gindin, Sergei I. "Obshchee i russkoe stixovedenie: Sistematicheskij ukazatel' literatury izdannoj v SSSR na russkom jazyke s 1958 po 1974 gg." In
Issledovanija [1410], pp. 152–222.

Lists 1,038 works; organized into 9 sections covering 1958–74; author and
subject indexes.

1339 ———. *Struktura stixotvornoi rechi: Sistematicheskiy ukazatel' literatury po ob-
shchemu i russkomu stixovedeniju, izdannoj v SSSR na russkom jazyke s 1958 g.
Chast' II: 1974–1980.* 3 parts. Moscow, 1982. 77 + 66 + 58 pp.

Extends the coverage in [1338] from 1974 to 1980.

1340 Lilly, Ian K., ed. *Russian Verse Theory Newsletter.* Auckland, N.Z.: Department of Russian, University of Auckland, 1983– (semiannual).

Current bibliography of works on Russian prosody; excludes other Slavic
traditions.

1341 Lilly, Ian K., and Barry P. Scherr. "Russian Verse Theory since 1960: A
Commentary and Bibliography." *International Journal of Slavic Linguistics and
Poetics,* no. 22 (1976): 75–116.

Surveys 283 works, 1960–73; discursive prefatory review followed by listings;
limited in subject to Russian verse but not limited to Soviet authors (as is
Smith below). Continued in [1342].

1342 ———. "Russian Verse Theory since 1974: A Commentary and Bibliography." *International Journal of Slavic Linguistics and Poetics,* no. 27 (1983): 127–
74.

Surveys 398 works, 1974–81; author index.

1343 Shtokmar, M. P. *Bibliografia rabot po stixoslozheniu.* Moscow, 1933.

Supplemented in *Literaturnji Kritik* 8 (1935): 194–205, 9 (1936): 235–53, and
by Roman Jakobson in his review in *Slavica* 13 (1934–35): 416–31.

1344 Smith, G. S. "A Bibliography of Publications on Russian Versification since
1958." *Russian Literature Triquarterly* 6 (1973): 679–702.

Lists 311 works; two indexes; limited to Soviet authors.

1345 Taranovsky, Kiril. "Metrics." *Current Trends in Linguistics, I: Soviet and East
European Linguistics.* Ed. Thomas A. Sebeok. The Hague: Mouton, 1963. Pp.
192–201.

Discursive survey of work since 1940.

ENCYCLOPEDIAS

1346 Terras, Victor, ed. *Handbook of Russian Literature*. New Haven: Yale University Press, 1985. 616 pp.

STUDIES

1347 Bailey, James. "The Basic Structural Characteristics of Russian Literary Meters." In *Studies Presented to Professor Roman Jakobson by His Students* [603], pp. 17–38.

1348 ———. "The Development of Strict Accentual Verse in Russian Literary Poetry." *Russian Literature* 9 (1975): 87–109.

1349 ———. "The Evolution and Structure of the Russian Iambic Pentameter 1880–1922." *International Journal of Slavic Linguistics and Poetics*, no. 16 (1973): 119–46.

1350 ———. "The Metrical Typology of Russian Narrative Folk Meters." *American Contributions to the Eighth International Congress of Slavists*. Vol. 1: *Linguistics and Poetics*. Ed. Henrik Birnbaum. Columbus, Ohio: Slavica, 1978. Pp. 82–103.

1351 ———. "Russian Binary Meters with Strong Caesura from 1890 to 1920." *International Journal of Slavic Linguistics and Poetics*, no. 14 (1971): 111–33.

1352 ———. "The Russian Linguistic-Statistical Method for Studying Poetic Rhythm: A Review Article." *Slavic and East European Journal* 23 (1979): 251–61.

1353 ———. "Some Recent Developments in the Study of Russian Versification." *Language and Style* 5 (1972): 155–91.

❖ Bailey, James [1035].

1354 Bely, Andrey. "Lirika i experiment." *Simvolizm*. Moscow, 1910. Trans. as "Lyric Poetry and Experiment" in *Selected Essays of Andrey Bely*. Ed. and trans. Stephen Cassedy. Berkeley and Los Angeles: University of California Press, 1985. Pp. 222–73.

1355 Bjorling, Fiora. "The Uses and Abuses of Syntax in Russian Modernist Poetry." *Russian Literature* 8 (1980): 499–551.

1356 Bobrov, Sergi. *Zapiski stixotvorce*. Moscow, 1916.

1357 Brik, Osip M. "Ritm i sintaksis" (1927); rpt. in *Two Essays on Poetic Language*. Postscript by Roman Jakobson. Ann Arbor: University of Michigan Department of Slavic, 1964. 81 pp.

1358 Bryusov, Valerij. *Osnov stixovedenija*. Moscow, 1924.

1359 Burgi, Richard. *A History of the Russian Hexameter*. Hamden, Conn.: Shoe String, 1954. 208 pp.

1360 Dłuska, Maria. *Studia z historii i teorii wersyfikacji polskiej*. 2 vols. Krakow: Polska Akademia Umiejetności, 1948–50.

1361 ———, ed. *Sylabotonizm*. Wroclaw: Zakład Narodwy im. Ossolińskich, 1957. 374 pp.

1362 Drage, C. L. "The Introduction of Russian Syllabo-Tonic Prosody." *Slavonic and East European Review* 54 (1976): 481–503.

1363 ———. "The Rhythmic Development of the Trochaic Tetrameter in Early Russian Syllabo-Tonic Poetry." *Slavonic and East European Review* 39 (1961): 346–68.

1364 ———. "Trochaic Metres in Early Russian Syllabo-Tonic Poetry." *Slavonic and East European Review* 38 (1960): 361–79.

❖ Eekman, Thomas [111].

1365 Eekman, Thomas, and Dean S. Worth, eds. *Russian Poetics: Proceedings of the International Colloquium at UCLA, 1975*. Columbus, Ohio: Slavica, 1983.

Fifteen essays on Russian versification.

❖ Elsworth, John [212].

1366 Erlich, Victor. "Verse Structure: Sound and Meaning." *Russian Formalism: History—Doctrine*. 3rd ed. New Haven: Yale University Press, 1981. Pp. 212–29.

1367 Etkind, E. *Materija stixa*. Paris: Institute d'Etudes Slaves, 1978. 506 pp.

1368 Garvin, Paul L., ed. and trans. *A Prague School Reader on Esthetics, Literary Structure, and Style*. Washington, D.C.: Georgetown University Press, 1964. 163 pp.

Introduction, eight essays, and bibliography.

1369 Gasparov, M. L. *Ocherk istorii russkogo stixa: Metrika, ritmika, rifma, strofika*. Moscow: Nauka, 1984. 319 pp.

1370 ———. *Sovremennyj ruskij stix: Metrika i ritmika*. Moscow: Hayka, 1974. 487 pp.

1371 ———, ed. *Russkoe stixoslozhenie XIX u: Materialy po metrike i strofike russkix poetov*. Moscow: Nauka, 1979. 453 pp.

1372 Gasparov, M. L. et al., eds. *Problemy stixovedenija*. Erevan: Izdvo Yerevanskago universiteta, 1976. 275 pp.

1373 Giergielewicz, Mieczyslaw. *Introduction to Polish Versification*. Philadelphia: University of Pennsylvania Press, 1970. 209 pp.

1374 Jakobson, Roman. *Early Slavic Paths and Crossroads*. Vol. 6 of his *Selected Writings*. 2 parts. Part 1: *Comparative Slavic Studies: The Cyrillo-Methodian Tradition*. The Hague: Mouton, 1985. Pp. 1–401. Part 2: *Medieval Slavic Studies*. The Hague: Mouton, 1985. Pp. 402–942.

1375   ———. *O cheshskom stixe.* 1932; rpt. in his *On Verse* [25], pp. 3–130.

1376   ———. "Slavic Epic Verse: Studies in Comparative Slavic Metrics." *Oxford Slavonic Papers* 3 (1952): 21–66; rpt. in his *Slavic Epic Studies.* Vol. 4 of his *Selected Writings.* The Hague: Mouton, 1966. Pp. 414–63.

1377   Jakobson, Roman, C. H. Van Schooneveld, and Dean S. Worth, eds. *Slavic Poetics: Essays in Honor of Kiril Taranovsky.* The Hague: Mouton, 1973. 574 pp.

❖   Janecek, Gerald [575].

1378   Kemball, Robin. "English and Russian Versification: A General Comparison." *Alexander Blok: A Study of Rhythm and Metre.* The Hague: Mouton, 1965. Pp. 55–156.

1379   Kopczynska, Zdzislawa, and M. R. Mayenowa. *Sylabizm.* Wroclaw: Zakład Narodwy im. Ossolińskich, 1956. 518 pp.

1380   Laferrière, Daniel. *Five Russian Poems: Exercises in a Theory of Poetry.* Englewood, N.J.: Transworld, 1977. 154 pp.

1381   ———. "Iambic Versus Trochaic: The Case of Russian." *International Review of Slavic Linguistics,* no. 4 (1979): 81–136.

1382   Levý, Jiří. *Paralipomena.* Brünn: Purkyne University, 1971. 113 pp.

His collected papers (six essays).

❖   Lotman, Jurij M. [42].

1383   Matejka, Ladislav, and Krystyna Pomorska, eds. *Readings in Russian Poetics: Formalist and Structuralist Views.* Cambridge, Mass.: MIT Press, 1971.

1384   Mukařovský, Jan. *The Word and Verbal Art.* Ed. and trans. John Burbank and Peter Steiner. New Haven: Yale University Press, 1977.

1385   Scherr, Barry P. "Rhyme"; "Syllabotonic Versification"; "Tonic Versification"; "Versification, Historical Survey of Russian." In Terras, ed. [1346], pp. 369–71, 458–60, 480–82, 504–8.

1386   ———. "Russian and English Versification: Similarities, Differences, Analysis." *Style* 14 (1980): 353–78.

1387   ———. *Russian Poetry: Meter, Rhythm, and Rhyme.* Berkeley and Los Angeles: University of California Press, 1986. 366 pp.

1388   Shaw, J. Thomas. *Pushkin's Rhymes: A Dictionary.* Madison: University of Wisconsin Press, 1974. 673 pp.

1389   Silbajoris, Rimvydas. "Syllabic versification." In Terras [1346], pp. 457–58.

1390   ———, ed. and trans. *Russian Versification: The Theories of Trediakovskij, Lomonosov, and Kantemir.* New York: Columbia University Press, 1968. 213 pp.

1391 Smith, G. S. "Bely's Poetry and Verse Theory." *Andrey Bely: Spirit of Symbolism.* Ed. J. E. Malmstad. Ithaca: Cornell University Press, 1987. Pp. 242–84.

1392 ———. "The Metrical Repertoire of Russian Emigré Poetry, 1941–1970." *Slavic and East European Review* 63 (1985): 210–27.

1393 ———. "The Metrical Repertoire of Shorter Poems by Russian Emigrés, 1971–1981." *Canadian Slavonic Papers* 27 (1985): 385–99.

1394 ———. "The Stanza Typology of Russian Poetry, 1735–1816: A General Survey." *Russian Literature* 13, no. 2 (1983): 175–203.

1395 ———, ed. and trans. *Metre, Rhythm, Stanza, Rhyme.* Colchester, Eng.: University of Essex Department of Language and Literature, 1980. 105 pp.

Introduction, 7 articles on Russian and English, bibliography.

1396 Stankiewicz, Edward. "Slavic [Versification]." In Wimsatt, ed. [60], pp. 89–99.

1397 Steiner, Peter. "Verse." *Russian Formalism: A Metapoetics.* Ithaca: Cornell University Press, 1984. Pp. 172–98.

1398 Taranovsky, Kiril. *Ruski dvodelni ritmovi.* Belgrade: Navchna knjiga, 1953.

1399 Timofeev, L. I. *Teorija stixa.* Moscow: Khudozhestvennaya literatura, 1939.

1400 ———, ed. *Russkoe stixoslozhenie: Tradicii i problemy razvitija.* Moscow: Nauka, 1985.

1401 Tomashevskij, B. V. *O Stixe: Stat'i.* Leningrad: Priboi, 1929.

1402 ———. *Russkoe stixoslozhenie: Metrika.* Petrograd, 1923; rpt. Munich: Wilhelm Fink, 1971.

1403 Tynjanov, Jurij. [Rhythm as the Constructive Factor of Verse.] In *Problema stixotvornogo jazyka.* Moscow, 1924. Trans. in *The Problem of Verse Language.* Ed. and trans. Michael Sosa and Brent Harvey. Ann Arbor: Ardis, 1981. Pp. 31–63.

1404 Unbegaun, B. O. *Russian Versification.* Oxford: Clarendon Press, 1956. 164 pp.

1405 Xolshevnikov, V. E. *Osnovy stixovedenija: Russkoe stixoslozhenie.* 2nd ed. Leningrad: Leningradskii gosudarstvennyi universitet, 1972.

1406 ———, ed. *Analiz odnogo stixotvorenija: Mezhvuzovskij sbornik.* Leningrad: Leningradskii gosudarstvennyi universitet, 1985. 248 pp.

1407 ———. *Problemy teorii stixa.* Leningrad: Nauka, 1984. 253 pp.

Seventeen essays and two bibliographies.

1408 ———. *Teorija stixa.* Leningrad: Nauka, 1968.

1409 Zhirmunskij, Viktor M. *Vvedenie v metriku: Teorija stixa*. Leningrad, 1925.
      Trans. C. F. Brown as *Introduction to Metrics: The Theory of Verse*. Ed. Edward
      Stankiewicz and W. N. Vickery. The Hague: Mouton, 1966. 245 pp.

1410 Zhirmunskij, V. M., D. C. Lixachev, and V. E. Xolshevnikov, eds. *Issledov-
      anija po teorii stixa*. Leningrad: Nauka, 1978. 232 pp.

      Nine articles and two bibliographies.

HEBREW AND ARABIC

HEBREW

❖ Baroway, Israel [777–78].

1411 Berlin, Adele. *The Dynamics of Biblical Parallelism*. Bloomington: Indiana
      University Press, 1985. 176 pp.

1412 Cobb, William H. *A Criticism of Systems of Hebrew Metre*. Oxford: Oxford
      University Press, 1905. 216 pp.

1413 Collins, Terence. *Line-Forms in Hebrew Poetry: A Grammatical Approach to the
      Study of the Hebrew Prophets*. Rome: Biblical Institute Press, 1978. 303 pp.

1414 Garr, W. R. "The *Quinah*—A Study of Poetic Meter, Syntax, and Style."
      Zeitschrift für die alttestamentliche Wissenschaft 95 (1983): 54–75.

1415 Gray, George Buchanan. Introduction. *The Forms of Hebrew Poetry*. London,
      1915; rpt. New York: Ktav Publishing House, 1972.

1416 Hrushovski, Benjamin. "Note on the Systems of Hebrew Versification." *The
      Penguin Book of Hebrew Verse*. Ed. T. Carmi. New York: Viking, 1981. Pp.
      57–72.

1417 Kugel, James L. *The Idea of Biblical Poetry: Parallelism and Its History*. New
      Haven: Yale University Press, 1981. 339 pp.

1418 Longman, T. "A Criticism of Two Recent Metrical Systems." *Biblica* 63
      (1982): 230–54.

1419 Lowth, Robert, Bishop of London. *De sacra poesi hebraeorum*. Oxford: Clar-
      endon Press, 1753. Trans. G. Gregory as *Lectures on the Sacred Poetry of the
      Hebrews*. 3rd ed. London, 1835.

1420 O'Connor, Michael P. *Hebrew Verse Structure*. Winona Lake, Ind.: Eisen-
      brauns, 1980. 629 pp.

1421 Robinson, Theodore H. "Basic Principles of Hebrew Poetic Form." *Fest-
      schrift Alfred Bertholet zum 80. Geburtstag*. Ed. Walter Baumgartner et al.
      Tübingen: J. C. B. Mohr, 1950. Pp. 438–50.

1422 Sievers, Eduard. *Metrische Studien I–III*. Leipzig, 1901–7.

1423 Tsur, Reuven. [Studies in Medieval Hebrew Poetry.] Tel Aviv: Daga, 1969. (In Hebrew.)

❖ Weinstock, Leo I. [173–74].

1424 Yoder, Perry B. "Biblical Hebrew [Versification]." In Wimsatt, ed. [60], pp. 52–65.

ARABIC AND SPANISH-ARABIC

1425 Bloch, Alfred. *Vers und Sprache im Altarabischen: Metrische und syntaktische Untersuchungen.* Basel: Verlag für recht und gesellschaft, 1946. 160 pp.

1426 Clarke, Samuel. *Scientia metrica & rhythmica, seu Tractatus de prosodia arabica.* Oxford, 1661. 170 pp.

1427 Compton, Linda F. *Andalusian Lyrical Poetry and Old Spanish Love-Songs: The Muwashshah and Its Kharja.* New York: New York University Press, 1976.

1428 Corriente, F. "The Meters of the Muwassah, An Andalusian Adaptation of Arud—A Bridging Hypothesis." *Journal of Arabic Literature* 13 (1982): 76–82.

1429 Freytag, Georg W. *Darstellung der arabischen Verskunst.* Bonn, 1830. 557 pp.

1430 Goldenburg, Yves. "La Métrique arabe classique et la typologie métrique." *Revue Roumaine de Linguistique* 21 (1976): 85–98.

1431 Hartmann, Martin. *Das arabischen Strophengedichte, I: Das Muwashshah.* Weimar, 1897.

1432 ———. *Metrum und Rhythmus.* Weimar, 1897.

1433 Hölscher, Gustav. "Arabische Metrik." *ZDMG* 74 (1920): 359–416.

1434 ———. *Syrische Verskunst.* Leipzig: J. C. Hinrichs, 1932. 206 pp.

1435 Kurylowicz, Jerzy. *Studies in Semitic Grammar and Metrics.* London: Curzon Press, 1973. 190 pp.

1436 Lasater, Alice E. *From Spain to England: A Comparative Study of Arabic, European, and English Literature of the Middle Ages.* Jackson: University Press of Mississippi, 1974.

1437 Latham, J. Derek. "New Light on the Scansion of an Old Andalusian Muwashshah." *Journal of Semitic Studies* 27 (1982): 61–74.

❖ Le Gentil, Pierre [487].

1438 Maling, Joan M. "The Theory of Classical Arabic Metrics." Diss., MIT, 1973.

1439 Martin, L'Abbé. *De La Métrique chez les Syriens.* Leipzig, 1879.

1440 Monroe, James T., and D. Swiatlo. "Ninety-three Arabic Hargas in Hebrew Muwashshahs: Their Hispano-Romance Prosody and Thematic Functions." *Journal of the American Oriental Society* 97 (1977): 141–63.

1441 Sammoud, Hamadi, and R. Ghozzi. "La Définition de la poésie dans l'ancienne poétique arabe." *Poétique*, no. 38 (1979): 149–61.

1442 Sowayan, Saad A. "Prosody and Language: A Synchronic and Diachronic Overview." *Nabati Poetry: The Oral Poetry of Arabia.* Berkeley and Los Angeles: University of California Press, 1983. Pp. 147–62.

1443 Sprengling, M. "Antonius Rhetor on Versification." *American Journal of Semitic Languages* 32 (1916): 145–216.

1444 Stern, Samuel M. *Hispano-Arabic Strophic Poetry.* Ed. L. P. Harvey. Oxford: Clarendon Press, 1974.

1445 Weil, Eliakim G. *Grundriss und System der altarabischen Metren.* Wiesbaden: Harrassowitz, 1958. 134 pp.

SANSKRIT AND PERSIAN

SANSKRIT

1446 Arnold, E. Vernon. *Vedic Metre in Its Historical Development.* Cambridge: Cambridge University Press, 1905. 335 pp.

1447 Fairbanks, Constance E. "The Development of Hindi Oral Narrative Meter." *DAI* 42, 10A (1982): 4452 (Wisconsin).

1448 Hopkins, E. Washburn. "Epic Versification." *The Great Epic of India: Its Character and Origin.* New York: Scribner, 1901; rpt. Calcutta, 1969. Pp. 191–362.

1449 Hudak, Thomas. "The Indigenization of Pali Meters in Thai." *DAI* 42, 6A (1981): 2652 (Michigan).

1450 Kiparsky, Paul. "Metrics and Morphophonemics in the *Rigveda.*" *Contributions to Generative Phonology.* Ed. M. K. Brame. Austin: University of Texas Press, 1972. Pp. 172–200.

1451 Lienhard, Siegfried. *A History of Classical Poetry: Sanskrit—Pali—Prakrit.* Part 1 of vol. 3 (*Classical Sanskrit Literature*) of *A History of Indian Literature.* Ed. Jan Gonda. 3 vols. Wiesbaden: Otto Harrassowitz, 1984. 307 pp.

1452 Oldenberg, Hermann. "Die Metrik des *Rigveda.*" *Die Hymnen des Rigveda.* 2 vols. Berlin, 1888. Vol. 1, pp. 1–190.

1453 Pollock, Sheldon I. *Aspects of Versification in Sanskrit Lyric Poetry.* New Haven: American Oriental Society, 1977. 335 pp.

1454 Vigorita, John F. "The Trochaic Gayatri." *Zeitschrift für vergleichende Sprachforschung* 93 (1979): 220–41.

1455 Warder, A. K. *Pali Metre: A Contribution to the History of Indian Literature.* London: Pali Text Society, 1967.

1456 Weber, Albrecht. *Über die Metrik der Inder.* Berlin, 1863. 484 pp.

1457 Weller, Hermann. *Anahita: Grundlegendes zur arischen Metrik.* Stuttgart: W. Kohlhammer, 1938.

1458 ———. "Beiträge zur Metrik des Veda." *Zeitschrift für Indologie und Iranistik* 1 (1922): 115–84.

1459 ———. "Metrica." *Beiträge zur indischen Philologie und Altertumskunde.* Hamburg: De Gruyter, 1951. Pp. 180–91.

PERSIAN

1460 Elwell-Sutton, L. P. *The Persian Metres.* Cambridge: Cambridge University Press, 1976. 285 pp.

1461 Farzaad, Masuud. *Persian Poetic Metres: A Synthetic Study.* Leyden: E. J. Brill, 1967. 128 pp.

1462 Heny, Jeannine M. "Rhythmic Elements in Persian Poetry." *DAI* 43, 1A (1982): 157 (Pennsylvania).

1463 Jones, Sir William ("Oriental"). "Of Versification" and "De Metris Asiaticis." In his *Works.* 13 vols. London, 1807. Vol. 5, pp. 300–319; vol. 6, pp. 22–59.

1464 Levy, Reuben. *Introduction to Persian Literature.* New York: Columbia University Press, 1969. Appendices.

1465 Meisami, Julie S. "Norms and Conventions of the Classical Persian Lyric: A Comparative Approach to the Ghazal." *Proceedings of the Ninth Congress of the International Comparative Literature Association.* 3 vols. Innsbruck, 1980–81. Vol. 1, pp. 203–7.

1466 Motamed, A. F. *De La Métrique.* Teheran: n.p., 1962. 133 pp.

1467 Thiesen, Finn. *A Manual of Classical Persian Prosody, with Chapters on Urdu, Karakhanidic, and Ottoman Prosody.* Wiesbaden: Otto Harrassowitz, 1982. 274 pp.

CHINESE AND JAPANESE

CHINESE

1468 Baxter, Glen W. *Index to the Imperial Register of Tz'u Prosody ... with a Bibliographical Note.* Rev. ed. Cambridge, Mass.: Harvard University Press, 1956. 61 pp.

1469 ———. "Metrical Origin of the *Tz'u.*" *Studies on Chinese Literature.* Ed. John L. Bishop. Cambridge, Mass.: Harvard University Press, 1966. Pp. 186–225.

1470 Birch, Cyril. "English and Chinese Meters in Hsü Chih-Mo." *Asia Major,* n.s. 8, no. 2 (1961): 258–93.

1471 Brooks, Bruce E. "Journey toward the West: An Asian Prosodic Embassy in the Year 1972." *Harvard Journal of Asiatic Studies* 35 (1975): 221–74.

1472 Frankel, Hans H. "Classical Chinese [Versification]." In Wimsatt, ed. [60], pp. 22–37.

1473 *Linguistic Analysis of Chinese Poetry.* Special Issue of *Journal of Chinese Linguistics* 8, no. 1 (1980).

      Eight essays and two discussions.

1474 Liu, James J. Y. "Auditory Effects of Chinese and the Bases of Versification." *The Art of Chinese Poetry.* London: Routledge & Kegan Paul, 1962. Pp. 20–38.

1475 ———. *Major Lyricists of the Northern Sung,* A.D. *960–1126.* Princeton: Princeton University Press, 1974.

1476 ———. "Technical Theories." *Chinese Theories of Literature.* Chicago: University of Chicago Press, 1975. Pp. 88–98.

1477 Nienhauser, W. H., Jr., C. Hartman, Y. W. Ma, and S. H. West. *The Indiana Companion to Traditional Chinese Literature.* Bloomington: Indiana University Press, 1986. 1050 pp.

1478 Ripley, Stephen A. "A Statistical Study of Tone Patterns in T'ang Regulated Verse." *DAI* 41, 5A (1980): 2115 (Toronto).

   ❖ Watson, Burton [515].

1479 Yip, Wai-lim. *Chinese Poetry: Major Modes and Genres.* Berkeley and Los Angeles: University of California Press, 1976.

JAPANESE

1480 Brower, Robert H. "Japanese [Versification]." In Wimsatt, ed. [60], pp. 38–51.

1481 Kodama, Sanehide. *American Poetry and Japanese Culture*. Hamden, Conn.: Archon, 1984. 264 pp.

1482 Miner, Earl. *Japanese Linked Poetry: An Account with Translations of Renga and Haikai Sequences*. Princeton: Princeton University Press, 1979. 376 pp.

1483 Miner, Earl, and Hiroko Odagiri. *The Monkey's Straw Raincoat and Other Poetry of the Basho School*. Princeton: Princeton University Press, 1981. 394 pp.

1484 Miner, Earl, Hiroko Odagiri, and Robert E. Morrell. "Literary Terms." *The Princeton Companion to Classical Japanese Literature*. Princeton: Princeton University Press, 1986. Pp. 265–305.

With useful introductory glossary.

AFRICAN

1485 Buning, T. *Afrikaanse Versbau*. Pretoria: J. H. de Bussy, 1939.

1486 Finnegan, Ruth. *Oral Poetry in Africa*. Oxford: Clarendon Press, 1970. 558 pp.

1487 Greenberg, Joseph H. "Hausa Verse Prosody." *Journal of the American Oriental Society* 69 (1949): 125–35.

1488 ———. "A Survey of African Prosodic Systems." *Culture in History*. Ed. Stanley A. Diamond. New York: Columbia University Press, 1960. Pp. 925–50.

1489 ———. "Swahili Prosody." *Journal of the American Oriental Society* 67 (1947): 24–30.

1490 Johnson, John W. "Somali Prosodic Systems." *Horn of Africa* 2, no. 3 (1979): 46–54.

1491 Lyonga, Nalova. "Literary Elements of African Oral Tradition in Modern Verse: Structure and Form." *Abbia* 34–37 (1979): 232–47.

1492 Okpeuho, Isidore. *The Epic in Africa*. New York: Columbia University Press, 1979.

1493 Rycroft, D. K. "The Question of Metre in Southern African Praise Poetry." *Third African Languages Congress of UNISA*. Ed. P. J. Wentzel. Pretoria: University of South Africa, 1980. Pp. 289–312.

1494 Shole, S. J. "Rhythm in Modern Setswana Poetry and How It Is Achieved." *African Languages* 1 (1981): 111–27.

INDEX

Abercrombie, Lascelles, 1033
Abernathy, Robert, 99
Abraham, Claude K., 1113
Adams, Joseph, 249
Adams, Kenneth, 1264
Adams, Percy G., 84
Adams, Stephen J., 999
Adler, Jacob H., 928
Adler, Jeremy, 555
Ahl, Frederick, 62
Aili, Hans, 179
Alden, R. M., 775–76, 1013
Alexander, Robert E., 585
Allen, Gay Wilson, 762
Allen, John D., 85
Allen, W. Sidney, 628–30
Alonso, Dámaso, 1265
Alpers, Paul J., 457
Amis, George T., 929
Anderson, Gary L., 153
Andrews, Bruce, and Charles Bernstein,
    eds., 300
L'Année Philologique, 614
Arnold, E. Vernon, 1446
Arnold, Matthew, 1000
Arts & Humanities Citation Index, 1
Atkins, Henry G., 1184
Attridge, Derek, 733, 1034
Austin, Timothy R., 250
Avalle, D'Arco Silvio, 1301
Aylward, Kevin H., 1001

Baehr, Rudolf, 1114, 1266
Baesecke, Georg, 1191
Bailey, James, 1035, 1347–53
Baker, William E., 251
Baldelli, Ignazio, 1302
Baldi, Sergio, 930
Baldwin, C. S., 692
Baldwin, T. W., 931
Bann, Stephen, ed., 570

Barber, Joseph A., 1303–4
Barkas, Pallister A., 992
Baroway, Israel, 777–78
Barry, M. Martin, Sister, 779
Barry, Peter, 154
Bate, W. Jackson, 780
Bateson, F. W., 868
Battaglia, Salvatore, 421
Baugh, Albert C., 869
Baum, Paull F., 180, 870, 1036
Bausinger, Hermann, 1192
Baxter, Arthur H., 734
Baxter, Glen W., 1468–69
Bayard, Carolyn A., 571
Beare, William, 8, 668
Beaver, Joseph C., 1070–72
Bec, Pierre, 489
Beccaria, Gian Luigi, 181, 1305–6
Belknap, George N., 368
Belmore, H. W., 1193
Beloof, Robert, 517
Beltrami, Pietro G., 1307–8
Bely, Andrey, 1354
Benedikt, Michael, ed., 586
Bennett, Charles E., 669
Bennett, W[alter], 735
Benot y Rodriguez, Eduardo, 1267
Bentley, Richard, 631
Berdan, John M., 781
Berghe, Christian L. van den, 1115
Berlin, Adele, 1411
Bernard, J. E., Jr., 782
Bernard, Suzanne, 587
Bernhart, Walter, 783
Bernheim, Roger, 469
Berry, Eleanor, 518
Berry, Francis, 252
Bers, Victor, 253
Bertinetto, P. M., 204, 1309
Bessinger, Jess B., Jr., 844
Beum, Robert, 100–101, 387, 784, 932

VERSEFORM

Designed by Chris L. Smith
Composed by BG Composition, Inc. in Bembo text and display
Printed by Edwards Brothers, Inc. on 50-lb. Glatfelter Natural and
bound in Holliston's Roxite B and stamped in pink and gold